# The Gallery Cat Caper

## A Klepto Cat Mystery

**Patricia Fry**

Matilija Press
PMB 123
323 E. Matilija St.,Ste 110
Ojai, CA 93023
www.matilijapress.com

# The Gallery Cat Caper

## A Klepto Cat Mystery
## by Patricia Fry

copyright © 2015 Patricia Fry

ISBN 978-0-9908313-8-9

This  novel is a work of fiction. The characters, names, incidents, dialogue are the products of the author's imagination or are used fictitiously. Any resemblance to actual persons, companies or events is purely coincidental.



Cover Art: Bernadette E. Kazmarski
Cover layout: Dennis Mullican
Page layout: Dennis Mullican

Printed in U.S.A. by: Create Space

**Other Novels by Patricia Fry**
CATNAPPED
Cat Eye Witness
Sleight of Paw
Undercover Cat
The Cat Colony Caper
Celebrity Cat Caper
The Corral Cat Caper
Mansion of Meows
Pawtners in Crime
Pawsitively Sinister
The Purrfect Lie

# The Gallery Cat Caper

## Klepto Cat Mystery—Book 8

"Well, I'll be…" Michael said, leaning back in his desk chair. "Savannah!" he called. "Can you come here for a minute?"

"Where are you?"

"Office."

"What?" she asked, appearing in the doorway with their baby in her arms.

"I can't believe this," he said, staring into the computer screen.

She moved closer.

"An old friend of mine just contacted me out of the blue. He wants to get together and catch up on all those years since college."

"How cool. Is it someone you'd like to reconnect with?" she asked.

He smiled up at her. "Sure would. I always wondered what happened to him." Michael took Lily from Savannah and lowered the baby onto his lap. He shook his head. "I can hardly believe it, but he's an artist, and apparently not the starving kind." After striking a few keys on the keyboard, he added, "Here, look at some of his work. It's really quite amazing."

Savannah leaned toward the computer screen. "Wow! That's stunning."

"There's more," Michael said, pulling Lily away from the keyboard with one hand and punching a few more keys with the other. "Look at this."

"Oh my gosh, is he ever talented!" She studied the paintings displayed on the page and said, "It's an interesting technique, isn't it? I mean, it's realistic, yet a touch whimsical." She stood straight and stared thoughtfully at the ceiling. "If his work is a reflection of the artist, I'd say he's playful, yet grounded, and extremely gifted."

"Yeah, you've pretty much pegged Peter Whitcomb. Except, when we were students, he wasn't doing art…that I know of." He rolled the office chair back a bit and looked up at his wife. "He has issued an invitation I'd really like us to consider."

"Oh?" Savannah said. She perched on the edge of the computer desk and waited to hear more. In the meantime, Michael pulled Lily back from the keyboard again and handed her a small plastic box of mints to play with. The baby shook the box vigorously and smiled.

"He has a gallery in a beach community down south of LA. He also owns a large home right on the sand." He hesitated before saying, "Savannah, he wants us to come down there this summer."

Savannah's face lit up. "My, my—does that sound inviting!"

"He said we could stay for a month if we want." He looked her in the eyes. "Imagine, summer at the beach. Oh, and he allows kids and pets. He has a dog and cats himself."

"Pets? How big is this place?"

Michael picked up the box of mints off the floor for the third time and handed it back to Lily. "Big enough for our family and some of our friends, if we want to bring anyone along."

"And this is Peter's home?" she asked.

"No. He lives someplace else. He rents the beach house out, but he's offering it to us for free." Michael reached for the box of mints again. Before he could give it to Lily, however, Savannah pulled a small stuffed doll out of her back pocket and handed it to her.

Michael smiled down at the baby, then said to Savannah, "There's just one caveat."

"Uh-oh," she said, narrowing her green eyes, "he wants us to paint the place?"

"No," Michael said, chuckling.

"He needs someone to care for his ailing grandmother?"

He laughed. "Savannah, no. Don't be silly."

"What then?"she asked, tilting her head, her highlighted blond hair flaring over one shoulder.

Michael thinned his lips before responding. "Well, he was kind of vague, but he seems to think someone's out to get him."

Savannah frowned. "He's being threatened?"

"I don't think so." He shook his head slowly. "It seems to be an attack on his work—his reputation. What he described to me sounds like sabotage…or he has become paranoid." He shrugged. "I don't know which."

"So we wouldn't be walking into a dangerous situation, right?" she asked.

"No. In fact, one of our classmates went into law enforcement. I think if Peter was concerned for his safety, he'd invite *him* to the beach, not a couple of veterinarians."

Savannah gazed at her husband and baby daughter. Finally, she asked, "When?"

Michael smiled up at her. "Pick a date, my dear."

"When can you get away from the clinic? How long are you thinking we'd be gone?"

Michael pondered the questions. "I'd like to take a real vacation, wouldn't you? Our vacations usually mean three days away—two of those traveling." He took her hand and asked, "How would you like to live at the beach for three weeks—or maybe longer?"

She took in a deep breath. "Gosh, that long?" She then relaxed a little, smiled, and said, "That might be wonderful, actually."

"Peter says they have concerts in a nearby park at night, he has a big art show coming up, the ocean's right in the backyard, and there's just a lot to do and see in the area. Maybe your mother would like to come and help out with the baby." He winked at her. "We could have a second honeymoon."

"Can you get away for that long?"

Michael nodded. "Sure; Bud's been practicing full-time long enough. He and the new tech should be able to handle our patient load without me. Hey, if your sister can leave her medical practice for a few days, maybe she'd like to spend some time with us. How long has it been since you and Brianna have frolicked on the beach together?"

Savannah clasped her hands in front of her and smiled. "That would be great fun."

Michael continued. "Bud might like to join us for a weekend, too."

"Oh, I'm sure they could use a vacation." She chuckled. "It's hard to imagine Bud at the beach, though; he's such a cowboy. But yeah, let's ask them. Will Ivey Veterinary Clinic survive with both veterinarians gone?" Michael thought about her question, then said, "I'll see if I can get Dr. Gladstone to take our emergencies. I helped him out last year when he and his wife toured Europe."

Savannah sat with her thoughts for a few moments, then said, "I'm flat-out speechless. It's so temping, but that's a long time to be away from the house, the orchard, the animals, our friends..."

"Everything's back to normal at Bonnie's stables since they nabbed the horse rustler. There's no reason why we can't board your horse there," he said. "Antonio can tend to the orchard. If a crop comes in while we're gone, maybe Helena and Antonio's wife could use it for jams and jellies."

"Yeah, that might work. I'd miss most of the apricot harvest. Some of the peaches and plums might ripen while we're gone, too. I'll invite Auntie and Colbi and maybe some members of the cat alliance to come pick what they want." Savannah reached out and petted the large grey-and-white cat, who had joined her on the desktop. "That just leaves the small animals. What will we do with them for an extended period?"

"Let's take them with us," Michael said, matter-of-factly.

She glanced at the cat and then at Michael. "Are you serious?"

*Meow!*

Michael laughed. "He seems to think it's a good idea, don't you, Rags?" He cleared his throat, then asked Savannah, "What do you think about us taking Adam? We've never gone to the beach with my son."

She smiled at the thought. "Oh, that's a great idea. He'd have a blast. Do you think Marci and Eric would let him go? Would there be room for all of our family, pets, and guests?"

"Heck, the place has something like five or six bedrooms and four baths. Peter told me it sleeps fifteen people—more if you bring sleeping bags. And it's all furnished, even with towels, sheets, blankets, pots and pans....and," he added, "a housekeeper."

"Gee, a beach mansion. This just gets more and more exciting, Michael. And having Mom there as a nanny—what a great idea. She would adore spending time with her only grandchild, and we could enjoy some nightlife."

"You got that right. I saw Peter's itinerary at his website. He's evidently involved in a lot of activities related to the arts—art shows, art walks, and things like that. That big show I mentioned is at a movie star's house. I forget who the actor is, but it sounds like a big deal." He reached out and squeezed Savannah's knee, saying, "So pack your little black dress and diamond earrings along with your bikini and sunscreen. We're going on vacation!"

***

A week and a half later, on Lily's six-month birthday, the Ivey family headed south in their SUV. Since Savannah often sat in the backseat with the baby, Lexie, their Afghan-hound-mix dog, was allowed to take Savannah's spot in the front. Rags, having become a seasoned road-trip traveler when he and Savannah were single, roamed free in the car. He spent most of the trip lying on the back of the seats, watching the scenery zoom past. When he wanted a nap, he stretched out in one of Buffy's pink canopy beds next to the large wire pen that the Himalayan-mix shared with their black cat, Walter. There was just enough room in the back of the SUV for extra water bowls, a litter box, and tote bags with necessary baby and pet supplies. They had rented a small trailer to carry the remainder of their belongings.

"When did you say Adam's coming?" Savannah asked.

"Marci and Eric will bring him Thursday. Tomorrow is his last day of school."

"They'll stay over with us, won't they? They aren't going to make that long trip down and back in one day."

"That's the plan," Michael said. He smiled. "I can't wait to boogie-board with my son." He glanced at Savannah in the rearview mirror. "Your mom's coming tomorrow?"

"Yes, in the afternoon. I'd like to get us settled first—have time to find where they keep the forks and spoons, whether we need to buy toilet paper—things like that." She reached out and petted Rags, who had jumped down next to her. "Bud and Bri are coming over the weekend. Oh, and Iris and Craig may possibly come for a few days. I finally got a strong *maybe* out of them. He's attending a seminar in Vegas next week, and they might drive over to the beach and spend a few days with us before heading home."

"Cool." Michael chuckled. "You have trouble visualizing Bud at the beach—what about Craig? Do you think he even owns a pair of swim trunks or board shorts? We see him only in his detective garb."

"We can always go shopping," she said, laughing.

"Hey, we've been on the road for five hours; are you hungry? Want to stretch your legs?" he asked.

"Yes, I think Lily's ready to be free of her restraints. Let's find a grassy area where we can eat our picnic lunch and let Rags and Lexie out. I brought harnesses for the other cats, but I'm not sure they'll wear them."

Michael switched on the blinker. "I'll bet we can find a picnic area around here somewhere. Let's ask when we get gas." He glanced at Savannah in the mirror again. "I put Walter's and Buffy's harnesses on a couple of times recently. They seemed okay with them. They were happier when I took them off, but they didn't really object to wearing them."

After filling the gas tank and driving a short distance, Michael pulled into a small park. "Perfect," Savannah said, looking around. She had already put Rags's harness on him. When they stopped, she led him out of the car and tied the long tether to a nearby tree. She poured him a bowl of water and placed some kibbles on a paper plate. In the meantime, Michael took Lily out of her car seat and carried her while walking Lexie on her leash to a dirt area away from the picnic tables. Savannah checked on the other cats. "Well, one of you used the litter box. Good girl—or boy," she said. She opened the door to the wire pen and invited the cats to step out and get a little exercise within the confines of the car.

She was standing at the picnic table unpacking the sandwiches, fruit, baby food, and water bottles when Michael returned saying, "Mission accomplished. Lexie is now at least two pounds lighter."

Savannah smirked at his humor. "Here, let me change her," she said, taking the baby from him and walking with her to the car. "Go ahead and eat your sandwich." She called over her shoulder, "There's hand sanitizer on the table."

Michael tied Lexie to a tree near Rags and showed her the water bowl, before washing his hands and unwrapping his sandwich.

In the meantime, Savannah changed Lily's diaper. "Hi Buffy," she said when she saw the fluffy buff-and-brown cat climb onto the back of the seat. Buffy stared down at the baby through clear blue eyes, then stepped into Lily's car seat and watched the diaper-changing process from there. Lily squirmed to see the cat, squealing with delight.

"You love your little Buffy, don't you, baby girl?" Savannah said, lifting the baby to a sitting position. "Yes, you love her almost as much as she loves you." She looked at the cat. "Do you want to go outside for a while, little one?" While Lily patted at the cat, who managed to stay just out of her reach, Savannah grabbed one of the leashes and snapped it to the harness she'd put on Buffy earlier. She then stepped out of the car with Lily in one arm and Buffy in the other.

"She probably doesn't need a leash," Michael said.

"Uh-uh. I'm not taking any chances with Buffy." She looked at Rags, who had walked around the tree so many times his tether was only a quarter of its original length. "Here Michael, would you hold the baby and Buffy? I need to untangle Rags."

"What about Walter?" Michael asked. "Doesn't he want to join us for lunch?"

"I don't think so. He's asleep in his tent. He looked at me, blinked, and laid back down. I guess he's not a road-trip guy."

Michael took Lily from Savannah. He put Buffy on the ground and stepped on her leash to keep her from wandering, then held the baby's little hand out of the way in order to take a bite of his sandwich without her grabbing it. "I guess this is what it would be like to have five kids," he said, after Savannah joined him at the picnic table. "Are you game?" he asked, smiling at her seductively

Savannah stifled a chuckle. "Let's see how this vacation goes, shall we?" she said, washing her hands and then opening a jar of strained pears for Lily.

After the lunch stop, Savannah and Michael loaded everyone back into the car and continued traveling south. It was dark by the time they reached Peter's house. They were surprised to find the porch light on and a glow emitting from behind the wood-slat blinds. "What a big place," Savannah said, staring out the car window at the massive structure.

"Wait here," Michael said, stepping out of the car.

Savannah watched as he slid the key Peter had sent them into the deadbolt lock. He tried to turn it and seemed to be having trouble. Suddenly, Savannah felt a surge of anxiety. *Oh gosh. What if we're at the wrong house?* she thought.

Within a few moments, however, Michael had the door unlocked. He walked back to the car, unbuckled the baby seat, and carried it—sleeping baby and all—toward the house. Savannah picked up her purse, stepped out of the car, and motioned for the dog to exit, as well. After locking the cats in the car, she led Lexie to a patch of grass where the dog promptly relieved herself.

"Did you think I had the wrong house?" he asked her, when she joined him at the front door.

"Yes, were you having trouble with the key?"

"Naw, I was just funnin' you."

"Michael, don't do that," she said, slapping at him.

"Hey, what are you trying to do, get a reputation for domestic violence our first few minutes in town?" he said, laughing.

Once inside the spacious living room, Michael set the baby seat down and Savannah closed the front door and locked it. "Wow," she said, as Michael began turning on lights in the dining room and kitchen. "This is kinda funky and rustic, but sure is big. Look at this kitchen! I could cook for twenty in here and serve them all at that monstrous table in the dining room."

"Let's look at the bedrooms," Michael said, taking her hand and leading her down a hallway. "Ordinary bedroom, ordinary bedroom…" he said as he poked his head into each room. "Oh, here's one with an ocean view—cool bedroom." Michael turned toward Savannah. "Let's go upstairs." After reaching the top landing, they walked into the first room on the left.

"This is gorgeous!" Savannah swooned. "Look at the exquisite furnishings."

"But wait, there's more," he said, leading her out the door to a room at the end of the hallway. "This one has an ocean view." He stepped over to a sliding glass door, unlocked it, and slid it open. "Check it out—a balcony overlooking the ocean."

"Wow!" Savannah said. "I can't see it, but I can hear it and smell it. Nice." She walked back inside and scanned the room. "Hey," she said, "here's an alcove just right for Lily. What's on the other side of it?" she asked quietly. She opened the door and exclaimed, "Another bedroom—with a view!" She looked around. "We can take the room with the larger balcony and attached bath, Mom can have this one, and we'll put Lily in the middle."

"Yeah," Michael said. "We'll all three have access to her, and our privacy, as well."

"That's what I was thinking," Savannah said, wrapping her arms around her husband's neck and kissing him.

He kissed her back a couple of times and then pulled away, saying, "We'd better unload the rest of the family." He yawned, and added, "…and get some sleep."

Savannah followed Michael back down the hall toward the staircase. "So that leaves rooms for Adam and one for Marci and Eric for one night. Bri and Bud can have Marci and Eric's room while they're here," Savannah calculated. "And if Craig and Iris make it, even if someone else is here, we still have plenty of room. This will work out just fine." As they made their way down the staircase, she said, "This place is great. I can't wait to see it in the daylight."

"So what do we absolutely need from the car tonight?" Michael asked, yawning again.

Savannah said, "The portable crib, the animals, the blue suitcase…actually, I'd like to bring it all in tonight. I don't want to leave it out there. We can stack it in the living room and deal with it in the morning."

"Okay. Help me unload the animals and you can get them settled while I bring in the rest of the stuff," Michael suggested.

After carrying in the last load, Michael locked the front door again, and Savannah began unpacking a few things while the three cats and the dog checked out their new surroundings. Soon, Michael came down the stairs. "The baby's asleep in her alcove—the little crib fit perfectly. Where shall we put the dog and cat beds?" he asked.

Savannah, hands on hips, looked around the large open living/dining rooms. "I'm thinking about putting Buffy's bed in the alcove with Lily. I'll take her water and kibbles bowls up and put them in our bathroom. How many litter boxes did we bring?"

"Three—you said you wanted three, right?" he asked.

"Right. So would you take one up for Buffy? I'll go find her and see if she likes her accommodations."

It didn't take long for Savannah to discover Buffy sitting on a windowsill in the dining room behind the blinds. "Come on, little one," Savannah cooed, as she picked up the Himmie-look-alike. Just then, Rags strutted in from the kitchen. He followed Savannah and Buffy up the stairs and spent the next several minutes becoming familiar with the scents and sights in their new bedroom. Evidently satisfied, while Buffy sipped water from her bowl, Rags sprawled across her pink canopy bed, which Savannah had placed near Lily's crib.

"Uh-oh," Michael said when he entered the room with a pan of litter.

"What?" Savannah asked, looking up from the task of hanging a few clothes in the closet.

"Your cat. He has claimed Buffy's bed again."

"Not to worry," she said, laughing. "I brought both of her beds. I guess I'll put the other one here in our room. Where are Walter and Lexie sleeping tonight?"

"I put their bowls and Lexie's bed in the service porch just off the kitchen. There was room for two litter boxes in the adjoining bathroom." He chuckled. "I imagine that bathroom is designated for beachgoers with sandy feet. Good place for a sandbox, don't you think?"

"Sure. Good job," she said flatly, in a weak attempt at humoring him. She then asked, "Where's Walter sleeping?"

"Oh, he discovered an afghan on a bed downstairs sort of like the one in that chair he likes in our living room. I found him sleeping under it."

Just then Savannah noticed something in Michael's hands. "What's that?" she asked.

"Peter left us a note. He says he'll be here at nine for breakfast—there's bacon, eggs, and fruit in the fridge." The two of them smiled at one another. "What a guy," Michael said. "Oh, and there's a concert tomorrow night in the park. He wants us to go with him."

"Sounds fun," Savannah said. "Okay, I think I have everything out that we'll need for this evening and tomorrow morning. I'll finish unpacking after breakfast."

***

The next morning, Savannah awakened to find herself, not only alone, but in a strange place. It took her a moment to get her bearings, but the first thing she did, after climbing out of bed, was to check on the baby in the alcove. *Gone! Michael must have taken Lily downstairs,* she thought to herself. She noticed that both of Buffy's beds were empty, too. She pulled back the lightweight nautical-print drapes and smiled upon seeing the ocean sparkling in the morning sun. *What a picture-perfect day,* she thought, walking out onto the balcony. Taking in a deep breath, she wrapped her arms tightly around herself, smiling in anticipation of the days ahead. *I'd better go see what my family's up to,* she thought, strolling back inside and entering the spacious bathroom. After freshening up, she slipped into her robe and headed out the door toward the staircase, hoping she could remember her way around the place.

Savannah was halfway down the stairs, when she heard voices. *Peter must be here.* She rushed back to her room and slipped into the capri pants and t-shirt she'd laid out for her first day of their beach vacation and then followed the sound of the voices into the kitchen. She approached Michael, who was sitting at the table holding Lily, and she kissed him. She then ran her hand along the baby's face and down one arm in a gentle caress.

"Hi hon," Michael said, looking up at her. "This is…"

Before he could finish, Peter turned away from the sink and said, "Well, hello there!" He walked toward Savannah drying his hands on a towel slung over one shoulder. "Savannah, right?"

She nodded and extended her hand. "And you must be our generous host. Nice to meet you, Peter."

Peter took her hand, lifted it gently, and gallantly kissed it, keeping his dark brown eyes on hers. He then said, "Michael, Michael. How do you do it, man? She's lovely."

Savannah looked at Michael, who was grinning proudly. She glanced back at Peter and said, "Thank you, kind sir."

He stared at her for a moment longer and then let go of her hand, saying, "Oh, I'm sorry. Didn't mean to attack you right out of bed. I hope you don't mind my barging in. Thought I'd fix you some breakfast."

"No, I don't mind. I'd welcome the Ninja Turtles if they were here to fix my breakfast," she said, chuckling.

Peter winked at Michael. "…and she has a sense of humor." He reached for the coffee pot and raised it toward Savannah. "Java?" he offered.

She noticed a pitcher of orange juice sitting on the table. "Is that fresh-squeezed?" she asked, pointing.

"Yep," Peter said. "Want some?"

She nodded, and he promptly removed a juice glass from the cupboard and filled it for her.

"Thanks," she said, taking Lily from Michael and snuggling with her.

Peter glanced from Michael to Savannah. "You make a beautiful family."

"Yes we do," Michael agreed, laughing.

"Where are the cats?" Savannah asked. "Have they come in for breakfast?"

Michael nodded. "I saw Buffy wandering around earlier. I know she ate. Walter is curled up with Lexie in there next to the washer and dryer."

"Really?" Savannah said. "I haven't seen those two share a bed in a while. Must be feeling a little insecure being in a new place and all." She looked around. "What about Rags? He's usually part of the breakfast crowd."

Peter turned away from the stove, holding a platter of bacon and eggs. "Oh, is that the large grey tuxedo cat?" he asked, walking toward the table.

"Yes. Have you seen him this morning?" Savannah asked, sipping her juice.

"Yeah, he went out when I came in."

Savannah choked and coughed. "He went out?" she nearly shouted.

Peter froze, a look of panic on his face. "Yeah, he isn't supposed to?"

"No," Savannah said, placing Lily in her bouncy chair. "Which door did he go out?" she asked, her voice raised an octave.

"Front," Peter said, watching her sprint past him. He turned toward Michael. "Gosh, I'm sorry. He looked so determined; I thought he needed a potty break."

"Yeah, he can be convincing," Michael said, taking his usual long strides into the living room after Savannah. Just as the two men caught up with her, they heard her exclaim, "Rags!" There he was, sitting on the front porch waiting for the door to open. Savannah hurriedly picked him up, wrapped her arms around him, and carried him into the house. "No, no," she said to him. "Don't you be tricking strangers into letting you out. Bad boy," she scolded, while holding him close.

"What's all this?" Peter asked, looking down at the porch and scratching his head.

"Close the door before the others get out," Savannah warned.

Peter stooped and picked something up. Carrying it inside, he closed the door behind him. "Michael," he said.

Michael glanced back at Peter, then took a double-take before saying, "Uh, hon, it looks like your cat's up to his old tricks."

When Savannah saw what Peter held in his hands, she closed her eyes and slumped a little. "Oh no," she groaned.

"What's wrong?" he asked. "Do you know where this stuff came from?"

"I'm afraid you turned a thief loose in the neighborhood, Peter," Michael said.

Their host looked confused. "What?"

"He takes things," Savannah said, placing Rags on the floor and watching him trot off toward the kitchen. "One reason he's not allowed out is because he's known to rob the neighbors blind."

"Oh my God. The cat went out and found this stuff and brought it back here?" He laughed. "I've never heard of such a thing." Peter looked down at the items in his hands. Then, dropping them on an ottoman, he said, "Let's see what he's got here. A grungy toy…" He picked up a dirty stuffed bear between the tips of his index finger and thumb. He glanced at the Iveys. "Maybe a dog toy." He shook his head in disbelief when he noticed a flip-flop among the items. He held up a piece of paper and laughed. "Hey, this looks like some kid's homework. How's he going to explain this to his teacher? 'The cat ate it,'" he mimicked. "Another toy," Peter said, lifting a small rubber duck out of the pile. And what's this?" he asked, laughing. He held it up for everyone to see. "A bathing-suit top? Man, that cat's a riot." He turned toward Rags, who was now sitting on the floor nearby watching the human activity. "Where did you get this, cat? Have you been undressing women on the beach?"

Savannah looked sullen. "Darn it, Rags. I thought you were reformed."

Peter continued to laugh. "So he has a record, does he?"

Savannah nodded. "You might say that. When we lived in LA, he used to bring all kinds of stuff like this home."

Michael interrupted, laughing, "And Savannah would pile it in a wagon and take it through the neighborhood on weekends, trying to find the owners. Get this, Peter," he said, "the cat would tag along with her."

Peter burst into laughter again. He looked at Rags, then asked, "He doesn't do it where you live now?"

Savannah shook her head. "Only because we don't let him out," she explained.

"He fleeces our guests, though," Michael said.

Peter looked at Michael and then Savannah. "Really? How does he do that?"

Michael grinned. "Just have a woman set her purse where he can get to it or leave your jacket somewhere and you'll find out."

Peter walked over to pet Rags. In turn, the cat bumped his head against Peter's hand.

"Oh great," Savannah said, chuckling, "he thinks you're complimenting him on his criminal behavior."

Peter glanced up at her. "Well, I am. I think he's awesome." He turned to Rags. "Yes, you're awesome, cat. You go guy," he said. He looked at his watch. "We'd better eat. I know you're on vacation, but I have to work this morning."

After breakfast, Peter rushed to leave. "Hey, come down and see my gallery when you get squared around," he invited. "And we'll have dinner tonight before the concert… on me."

"Dinner on you?" Michael questioned. "I don't remember that happening when we were in college." Michael patted his friend on the back. "You're not the typical starving artist, are you, Peter?"

"No, fortunately, I'm not." He looked down. "But sometimes success can be as much a burden as failure can."

"What? Why?" Michael asked.

He became sullen. "It can make you a target." Then he smiled. "Oh, never mind that. You're on vacation. You two have fun." He looked at Savannah. "I gave Michael directions to the gallery. Hope to see you all later."

"Sure; and thanks for breakfast." Once Peter had left, Savannah suggested, "Let's finish our coffee on the deck and watch the waves, want to?"

Michael nodded. He picked up Lily in her chair, saying, "We're gonna go check out the beach, baby girl."

Just then, Rags jumped up on the kitchen table and began dancing around, making kitty prrrrt sounds.

"No, Rags. You're on time-out. No beach activities for you this morning," Savannah said while filling their coffee mugs.

When Rags reached out with one paw toward Michael, he said, "Sorry buddy, what Mom says goes. You're sitting this one out."

Just then, they noticed Lexie dancing around Michael's feet. "Yes, you can come out, girl," he said. "Savannah, would you get her leash?"

"Gosh this is the way to live, isn't it?" Michael said, once they'd settled into cushioned deck chairs under the shade of an over-sized umbrella.

"Yes, what a view. And it's so cool that there are options here on the deck," she said, motioning with her arms, "…plenty of shade or full sun. I could sure get used to this—and having someone fix breakfast for us…that was a nice surprise." She became thoughtful for a moment and said, "I think he's lonely."

"Who?" Michael asked, peering at her over his sunglasses.

"Your friend, Peter."

"Why would you say that? He's got everything—money, talent…fans… It sounds like he has a lot of friends and quite a social life."

"Oh, I don't know. Just seems like something's missing for him. Maybe it's my imagination." She handed Michael her phone. "Here, take a picture of Lily and me with the ocean in the background" After looking at the resulting photograph, she said, "I'm sending this to Iris, Colbi, Craig, Bri, Bonnie…oh, someone's calling. It's Mom." She put the phone up to her ear. "Hi, Mom "

"Hi honey. Are you at the beach?"

"Yes. It's a great place. Wait 'til you see it."

"How long will you and Michael be staying?"

"We're playing it by ear, but maybe as long as three weeks. Can you believe it?"

Gladys's voice cracked a little. "Oh, that would be wonderful."

"How far away are you from here, Mom; an hour?"

"About that, depending on traffic. Forty minutes on a good day."

"So what time will you come and how long can you stay?" Savannah smoothed Lily's hair. "Your granddaughter's eager to see you."

"Oh, I can't wait to see that darling child. I have an appointment this morning. I'll be there after lunch. I thought I'd pack for a week and see how it goes. I can always run home if I need to."

"Super. If we're not here, we'll leave a key under the mat. You have the directions and the address, right?"

"Yes," Gladys said. "…all punched into my GPS. See you later. Oh, how about if I fix fried chicken for dinner?"

"Maybe tomorrow, Mom. We've been invited out tonight. If you don't mind, I thought you and Lily could hang out here. Michael and I don't get a date night very often."

Gladys didn't hesitate before saying, "That would be great. I look forward to it."

***

"Hello!" Michael called, as he entered Peter's gallery with Savannah and Lily later that morning. "Anyone here?"

Peter stepped out from behind one of several panels of art and joined them in the main gallery. "Hi," he said, running one hand through his dark, curly hair. "Out slumming?" he asked, chuckling, his brown eyes glistening against his tanned complexion.
"So this is where it all happens, huh?" Michael asked.

"It's wonderful," Savannah said. "Seeing your art in person is even more exciting than seeing it at your website."

Peter smiled. Bowing graciously, he said, "Well, thank you. Hey, come look around," he invited, walking between some of the exhibit panels. Michael followed with Lily in her stroller, while Savannah hung back, staring at a painting that had attracted her attention.

*There's so much to each of his pieces,* she thought. *The more you look, the more you see. Oh, there's a cat. I wonder how many people notice the cat crouched there near that tree. He has such a unique quality to his work. Makes you want to know more about the artist. I can see why he gets so much attention.*

Suddenly she heard Michael call out to her. "Savannah, you've gotta see this."

"Coming," she said, as she headed in the direction of his voice. *Where are they?* she wondered. *There sure are a lot of nooks and crannies in this place. Oops, this must be his office.* She started to back out, when a painting on the opposite wall caught her eye. *Wow, that's a great painting,* she thought. She couldn't help herself. She walked toward it and, for a moment, felt as if she had become part of it. *"Forest Folly,"* she read. *It's interesting how his paintings tend to draw you in.*

"Savannah, are you lost?" Michael called. "Oh, there you are," he said, peering into the office. "I want you to see something."

As she turned to follow him, he disappeared from view. In her haste to catch up, one of her flip-flops caught on the leg of the office chair and she stumbled forward, catching herself with her hands on the desktop. "Klutz," she whispered. She started to walk away when she stopped. *Who's that?* she wondered, studying the small window in front of her. Within seconds the image disappeared. *Was that man watching me?* She moved toward the window and peered out. *I guess he's gone. Maybe he was just walking past.* She stopped and thought about it for a moment and then said to herself, shuddering, *Sure seemed as though he was staring into this room.*

"Savannah, what are you doing?" Michael called. "Are you lost again?"

"No, I'm coming," she said. She glanced at the window again and shook her head as she exited Peter's office. When she finally caught up with the others, Michael pointed to a series of framed articles featuring Peter and his work, which had been published in some of the most prestigious magazines in the art world.

"Wow!" Savannah said. She turned to Peter. "Impressive. I love your work. I'm no art connoisseur, but I know what I like." She motioned toward the articles and chuckled. "Obviously I'm not the only one." She thought for a moment and then added, "Your paintings have such depth. They're realistic, yet whimsical and full of surprises. I'm definitely taking one home with me—even if it's just a print. Not sure I can afford the real thing. You're too famous for my pocketbook," she said, laughing.

Peter smiled. "Every artist loves a positive critique."

"You can't possibly get anything else," Michael said.

"Well, you wouldn't think so. But I can tell you, the bigger you become, the larger target you are." He took in a breath and ushered the couple back toward the main gallery. "But enough about me. What's on your agenda today?"

"Just looking forward to the concert tonight. We even have a babysitter," Michael said, "which is rare."

"Other than that, we're content to just watch the surf and the people. This is a great people-watching place."

"Oh yeah," Peter agreed, winking.

Just then a young woman in her twenties walked into the gallery wearing a pert red-and-white polka-dot dress and casual sandals. She slipped on a red shrug as she entered. "Hi," she said, flashing a demure smile exposing straight, slightly over-whitened teeth. "The wind's picking up," she said, pulling strands of her short auburn hair back into place with her fingers.

*Love that sassy hairdo,* Savannah thought. *It's a perfect frame for her pretty face. Her blue eyes literally sparkle under those feathered bangs. Maybe I should consider…*

Peter's voice interrupted her thoughts. "Here's my top sales executive," he said, smiling at the young woman. "Kara, meet my friends, Michael and Savannah Ivey and the little Ivey, makes three," he said in a sing-song manner.

Everyone laughed. Michael and Savannah greeted Kara as Peter continued the introduction: "Michael and Savannah are here visiting from Northern California." He put his arm around the young woman's shoulders. "Kara works here part-time. She's a college student studying art. She's wonderful with customers—knows how to make that sale."

Kara shook her head and smiled. "There's no selling to Peter's art. You see it; you want it."

"You've got that right," Savannah said. "I was just telling Peter I'm a soon-to-be owner of his work. Just have to figure out which one I want to take home."

Peter grinned at her and then turned to Kara. "Now that you're here, I'm going to leave for a while. I'll be back in an hour or so. Come on," he said to Savannah and Michael, "I'll show you where I live, when I'm not at the gallery or traveling."

"Nice to meet you, Kara," Savannah said, as she trailed after the men toward the front door. But the girl didn't seem to hear her. *What's got her intense attention?* she wondered, following Kara's gaze. *She's staring at Peter. Hmm, he didn't notice.* When Savannah stepped out onto the sidewalk, she glanced back at Kara through the window. *Looks like she has a crush on her boss, or is that an expression of hostility? Hard to tell. Whatever her feelings, they're intense.*

"You say you work in a loft?" Michael asked, as they strolled away from the gallery past quaint shops filled with everything imaginable related to the beach. Savannah noticed several stores offering local art of all kinds—from hand-painted seashells and jewelry to metal art and screen-printed clothing to note cards and sculpted sea creatures.

"You're lagging," Michael called out to Savannah.

"There's a lot to see," she explained.

"Yes, there is," Peter agreed, twisting his head to ogle a couple of bikini-clad women.

"You haven't changed a bit, have you, Peter?" Michael said, laughing. "Still watching skirts."

"What skirts?" Peter asked, turning and winking at Savannah, who was rushing to catch up.

"Peter," Savannah said in hushed tones," do you know that man over there?"

"Huh? Where?" he asked.

"Oh, he's gone," she said, attempting to spot him again.

"Who was it?" Peter asked.

"Well, I saw him earlier outside your office window. Just now, it appeared that he was watching us."

Peter squinted. "What did he look like?"

"Kind of scraggly. He had unkempt medium-brown hair and a beard. He was wearing a baseball cap."

Peter chuckled. "Sounds like any one of the homeless who hang around this area. You've also described some of the typical surfer dudes."

"Well, this one seemed interested in us," she said.

"Savannah, do you mean to tell me that you don't get looks when you walk down the street in Hammond?" he asked, grinning.

"No, Peter," she said. "Not like that. This guy had something else on his mind."

"Oh, so he was interested in us guys?" Michael asked, laughing.

"No. Just never mind," she said, pouting a little. "If some creepy guy jumps out of the bushes and knocks you over the head with his skateboard, just remember that I tried to warn you."

By then, they were walking away from the beach and the shopping district.

"So you don't live on the beach," Michael remarked.

"No, but I can enjoy the ocean from where I am." He pointed. "See the third house up the hill there? …that pukey-yellow and poopy-brown monstrosity?"

"Yes," Michael said, frowning.

Savannah nodded, her eyes wide.

"That's not it," Peter said. "I'm at the top of the street in the Cape Cod. See the telescope in the bay window?"

Michael looked at Peter. "A loft in a Cape Cod?"

Peter shrugged. "What can I say; I'm an artist." He turned to Savannah, who was walking alone behind them and asked, "Is the baby enjoying the beach?"

"Well, we haven't had her down on the beach yet," she said. "I'm not sure she'll like the feel of the sand or the cold ocean water. Tomorrow's our beach day."

"Oh yes, my son's coming tomorrow," Michael said, excitedly. "Wait 'til you meet him. He's quite a boy." He turned to Peter. "You never had any children, did you? Ever marry?" he asked.

Peter was silent for a few seconds, then, ignoring the questions, he said, "Here we are; home. Come meet my family."

Savannah and Michael exchanged looks—wondering who might lurk behind the cobalt- blue door. Using a key, Peter opened the door a crack and looked around. "The coast is clear," he said. "Come on in."

"What do you mean 'the coast is clear'?" Michael asked, maneuvering the stroller into the room. "What were you expecting to see—a date leftover from last night?"

Peter raised his eyebrows. "You never know, Michael, you old married man, you."

Savannah entered last and closed the door just as a wooly husky wriggled happily into the room toward them. "Hi, Sakari," Peter said. "Come meet some new friends."

"Sakari?" Savannah repeated. "A Japanese name for an Alaskan husky? Or is she Siberian?" she asked.

"Long story. Actually, she's a mix of Alaskan and Siberian and the name comes from Alaska. My fiancé called her 'Sweetie.' When she left and I took my manhood back..." he chuckled, "I started calling her Sakari, which, I must admit, still means *sweet*, but it doesn't sound so foo- foo."

"Well, she *is* sweet," Savannah said, kneeling to pet the rambunctious dog. When Sakari danced her way toward Michael for some petting, Savannah stood and looked around. "Great house. Do you do a lot of entertaining?" she asked.

"As little as possible. But it kind of comes with the territory. When you have a big house, you're often elected to host events."

"I know what you mean," Savannah said. "We have a big old house that Michael has been refurbishing little by little and, since we have the room, any gatherings are usually at our place. We've hosted weddings, charity events, most of our organization meetings..."

Peter nodded. "I hear ya. That's what people expect, isn't it?" He addressed Michael, "You're a handyman?"

"Yes, you might say that's my art," he said, faking a pretentious air.

Peter hesitated for a moment. In a more serious tone, he said, "Well, I might have a project for you."

"Anything I can do to help," Michael said. "Do you have tools?"

"Uh, no," he lowered his head. He then perked up and said, "But I know someone who does."

Michael shook his head, lowering his brows. "Guys don't like to loan their tools, Peter. A man's tools are like... well, probably like your paint brushes and paints...sacred... off-limits..."

Peter looked at him, nodding silently. He then took a breath, which seemed to give him a spark of energy. "Well, let me give you the grand tour. I'll explain what I need and we'll see what we can figure out."

Michael lifted Lily out of the stroller and carried the sleeping baby in his arms as Peter walked them through the house. "This is the kitchen, where I spend the least of my time." He opened a large pantry. "See, nearly bare. I'm no fan of cooking."

"Well, you're pretty good at it," Savannah said. "Your breakfast was delicious."

"Oh, that was a fluke. Beginner's luck. I eat out a lot," he admitted. He smiled. "But I do get regular home-cooking. I have a wonderful housekeeper who pampers me with great meals. She actually cooks while she cleans. So on the days she comes, I look forward to a real dinner, as well as sweet rolls or muffins for breakfast the next day." He faced Michael and Savannah. "Hey, you'll meet her; she cleans the beach house on Fridays, if you don't mind her coming in."

Savannah shook her head.

"Ah yes, what would I do without Mama Maria?" he said, smiling. He then frowned. "I hope I don't have to find out. Lately, she's been a little spooked. I'm not sure she can hang in there with all that's going on."

Before Michael or Savannah could respond, Peter hastened his gate toward a narrow staircase to the right of the kitchen. "Come see my studio."

The staircase led to a large loft overlooking the spacious living room and with views of mountains on one side and the ocean on the other.

"Wow!" Savannah said, looking around. "What a bright, welcoming place."

"Yes, isn't it?" Peter agreed.

She walked over to a long table against the only wall without windows and looked at Peter's array of paints, brushes, and other items she guessed were used in his art. "You frame your own paintings?" she asked when she spotted an orderly supply of framing materials.

"I do some. I have a gal who comes in and builds frames for me a few times a week. Charlynn does a good job."

"Is this your current project?" Michael asked, viewing the canvas resting on an easel.

"One of them," he said. "I paint by mood."

"By mood? Oh, that's interesting," Savannah said. Suddenly, she faced him. "Please tell me you're not a Gemini."

"Uh, why?" he asked.

"Gemini's are probably the most moody of all with their twin personas."

"Well, I'm not a Gemini. I'm a Cancer—on the cusp of Gemini."

"Yikes! Even worse!" Savannah said.

"Do you believe in all that stuff?" he asked her.

"Oh, it's just a fascination for me. I don't really know much about astrology." She looked at Peter. "Evidently, you're using the best of all aspects of your chart because you seem to be doing very well." Savannah glanced around at the paintings. Suddenly she was drawn to one of them. "Who did this one?" she asked, studying it more closely.

"That's mine," Peter said quietly. "Why?"

She looked at him and then at the painting. Stepping back, she viewed it from a different angle. She shook her head slowly. "It isn't…well…it's different than the others. It's dark."

Peter studied Savannah's face. He finally said, rather flippantly, "How astute of you, young lady. That was… well, I wasn't in a good place when I did that one. I wanted to paint over it, but decided the mood—the emotion—was something I needed to face." He took in a deep breath. "If I'm going to stay in this business and enjoy the status I've achieved, I guess I need to develop a tougher outer core."

Savannah glanced at Michael, who was examining the framing equipment while still holding their sleeping child. She then looked back at the painting. "Sad," she said.

"Sad?" he asked.

"I sense sadness in this piece."

"Well yeah," Peter said, grinning, "the tree branches are drooping, the raindrops look like teardrops, the colors are drab. There's no joy there—even the creatures are hiding from the light; see the fox in the burrow? Look at his eyes. And the birds… I painted birds in this one—even they don't look happy, right?"

"Interesting," Savannah said. "I sensed it—I felt it—but I couldn't describe it."

"You have a good eye for the emotion in art—at least my art." His demeanor brightened as he walked briskly to the other side of the room. "Come look at this one. What emotion is prevalent here?" he asked.

Michael joined Peter and Savannah in front of the painting. He poked his wife playfully in the ribs. "What are you, an art critic now?"

"She's pretty good at it," Peter said. "Now what is the emotion here?" he asked her. "Can you feel it or sense it?"

Savannah gazed at the large painting. Finally, she said, "Wow! What comes to me is conflict, maybe confusion."

Peter looked at Savannah. Finally, he said, "I was at a crossroads in my life and in my art when I painted it." He reached behind it. "Here's a print of the one I did after the conflict was…pretty much resolved. I've sold more copies of this print than probably any other. Can you see the emotionally-driven changes in my work between these two?"

"Oh yes," Savannah said. "That's when the playful, whimsical aspect appeared…or returned, maybe."

Michael walked closer to the paintings Savannah and Peter were comparing. He looked from one to the other and said, "I can't see much difference. They're both really good."

"The differences are subtle, Michael," Peter explained. "You have to be able to feel what's in the strokes and the colors. Savannah has an uncanny ability to do that." He turned to her. "Where did you get that skill?"

She shrugged. "Heck, I didn't know I had it."

"She's as intuitive as most cats," Michael said. "I don't know how she comes up with some of the things she does." He then said, "I think I could paint a picture in this environment. Is this the only place you paint? Is this where you get your inspiration?"

"Once you've painted as long as I have, you don't need outside visual stimulation. It comes from inside." Peter looked somber. "And that's what people don't understand. You can't force or manufacture this," he said, moving his arm in a sweeping motion toward the array of his paintings.

"Certainly not," Savannah agreed. "Does someone think they can?"

Peter let out a sigh. "Apparently." His demeanor suddenly brightened. "Come on, I have something else to show you," he said, leading the Ivey family down the stairs, through a long hallway, and into the garage.

"Nice cars," Michael said, once the garage light went on.

"That's not what I want to show you. But yeah, I do enjoy my cars. He pointed to a low, lean sports car and smiled. "I use this one to get the girls—I mean women," he said with a chuckle. He nodded toward a shiny black sedan.

"The luxury car's for dating."

Michael shook his head. "Peter, Peter…what a life you lead."

"Yeah, I know—you're envious, right?"

Michael put one arm around Savannah. "Not really," he said, shaking his head slowly.

Peter walked past the cars to another door and invited the couple to follow him. They exited onto a lovely patio with a high wall around it. "Let's see," he said glancing around the area. He pointed toward a gathering of pots filled with colorful flowers. "There's Gingersnap. And Claude is lying on the other side of those petunias."

"Geraniums," Savannah corrected.

"What?" Peter said, looking confused. "Oh, yeah, the flowers. I call all flowers petunias." He gazed in that direction again. "Those aren't petunias?"

Savannah stooped and petted both cats. "They're really cute. Are they siblings?"

Peter appeared stunned. "How did you know that?" he asked. "They look nothing alike."

"They look a lot alike," Savannah said. "One's bigger, but they have the same facial structure, same ears, same cobby body, fur is similar…"

"Oh, I never noticed that. I just noticed they're different colors and they have different personalities."

"Yes, Gingersnap is an orange tabby and Claude is a tuxedo cat—way different coloring, but very similar body types and features."

Peter walked over to the two young cats. "Never noticed that before."

"So do they roam?" Savannah asked.

"No," Peter said, emphatically. "See that wire around the top of the wall?"

"Yes, electric, huh?"

"You electrocute your cats?" Michael asked.

"No. I turn it on at a real low voltage for about a week when I get a new cat. Then I don't need it anymore. The cats know they're supposed to stay inside. You probably saw the pet door from the house into the garage and the one out to here. The cats and dog have the run of the place, only I close this door off at night."

"Don't want a seagull to get them, huh?" Michael laughed.

Peter nodded. "Something like that."

"So what's the job you want to show me, Peter?" Michael asked.

He took in a deep breath. "I'd like to put in some cameras."

"Surveillance cameras?" Michael asked. "Out here? Also maybe in front of your garage, right?"

"No, inside," Peter said. "Here in my studio and at the gallery."

"Why inside?" Michael asked, creasing his brow.

Peter looked at Michael and then Savannah. "Man, I don't want to drag you into this. Probably should have put off your visit—but…" Just then Peter's cell phone rang. He edged it out of his jeans pocket, looked at it, and said, "I'd better take this call."

Michael glanced at Savannah and then back at Peter. "Uh, okay, we should go get something to eat anyway, and Savannah's mother's coming in this afternoon."

"See you tonight? Meet me at the gallery at seven, and we'll go from there." He addressed Savannah. "Dress is casual; probably get a little chilly tonight." He started to put the phone up to his ear, but stopped and asked, "Can you find your way back to the living room?" He pointed. "Just head that direction, through the door. See you later," he called after the couple as they walked away.

"Whew, that was quite a walk up this hill, wasn't it?" Savannah commented as they stepped out the front door and started down the steep driveway.

"Going down with the stroller isn't much easier than it was pushing it up," Michael said. "I think if we visit Peter's home again, we'll drive."

Savannah shuddered. "I'm a little leery about visiting him."

"For heaven's sake, why?" Michael asked.

"It sounds like he has someone after him. He seems a little nervous. Even his housekeeper's frightened," Savannah said.

"Wouldn't you be concerned if you had so much at stake?" Michael asked. "The bigger you get, the more you have at risk and the more you fear losing it."

"Michael, I don't care how big or small you are. No one wants to lose what they have." She looked at him. "Maybe he's paranoid. Have you known him to overreact to things before?"

He thought for a moment before saying, "No. In fact, he was always the cool guy—nothing fazed him."

"Well, something seems to be *fazing* him, now. I'm curious to know what it is."

The couple walked in silence for a block and then Michael said, "It is odd that he wants cameras installed inside, don't you think? Maybe he's worried about people stealing his art. You know, his gallery is certainly attractive, but the design isn't very practical. There are a lot of areas hidden from view. It would help if he'd cut those aisle panels down so there's more visibility around the room."

Savannah nodded. "I can understand why he installed tall ones—they show off his larger paintings better. I agree that the design of the gallery sort of lends itself to thievery. But I don't think that's why he wants the cameras."

"Oh?" Michael said. "Why, then?"

"There may be someone close to him that he doesn't trust."

Michael thought about that for a minute and then said, "Or maybe he doesn't know who he can and can't trust."

## Chapter 2

An hour later, Savannah and Michael were sitting on the deck of the vacation beach house, looking out over the ocean and eating turkey sandwiches they'd picked up from a nearby deli, when Savannah suddenly gasped. She sat forward in her chair and pointed. "Look, Michael! Look!" she said.

Michael squinted in the direction she pointed, then glanced back at her. "What?"

She walked to the edge of the deck and called to someone on the beach below. "Hey, wait a minute!" Once Savannah had attracted the young woman's attention, she motioned for her to come closer. The twenty-something-year-old woman and her male companion walked cautiously toward Savannah, both of them shading their eyes from the sun with their hands.

Savannah cupped her hands around her mouth and shouted over the sound of crashing waves, "I think I have something of yours!"

The couple looked at one another and then back at Savannah and continued walking slowly toward the deck.

"Wait there," Savannah said, before rushing into the house. When she returned, she carried a bikini bathing-suit top. "Is this yours?" she asked, holding it up.

The woman looked confused. She walked closer to the deck and nodded. "Yes." She peered suspiciously at Savannah. "Where did you…? I mean, how did it…?"

"If I tell you, you won't believe it," Savannah said, chuckling.

The woman cocked her head. "Try me. I'm curious. I've been looking everywhere for this." She motioned toward her companion, giggled, and said, "I even accused him of hiding it."

Savannah leaned over and handed the top to her, saying, "Well, I have this cat…"

"Cat?" the woman questioned.

"Yes, he…well, he takes things. He escaped from the house this morning and came home with a bunch of stuff, including your top."

Michael walked closer to where Savannah stood. "Do you live near here?" he asked the other couple.

"Let's see…" The woman looked up the beach, began counting houses, and said, "…we're staying in the fourth house up. I left my suit on the deck last night to dry, and this morning the top was gone."

The tall, slim man with her said, "I figured the wind carried it away. But a cat…?" He looked beyond Savannah and pointed. "That cat?"

Savannah and Michael glanced toward the sliding doors. Both of them nodded. "That's the culprit," Michael said.

The young woman moved forward to get a closer look. "He takes things, huh?"

"Yes, he's a terrible kleptomaniac," Savannah said. "That's one reason he's not allowed outside anymore. He sneaked out this morning without us knowing."

"But grounding him doesn't help," Michael said. "Now he robs our guests blind."

Savannah nodded. "That's right; we have to hide their jackets and purses."

"He steals from your guests?" the man asked. "Sounds like he needs something to keep him out of trouble—a hobby, perhaps," he joked, laughing.

"Well, he has a job," Michael said, straight-faced.

The man scrutinized Rags. "Is that right?"

"Yes, he's a detective for the local sheriff's department in our hometown," Michael explained. He chuckled. "They say he's the best snitch they have."

"Rags!" the woman shouted, her face lighting up. "I've read about him," she said, excitedly.

Savannah and Michael exchanged glances. "You have?" she asked. "Where?"

"Oh, there was something about him on one of the animal websites I visit. I don't remember which one. I was fascinated by his story."

"Well, we were interviewed not too long ago by a reporter," Savannah said. "Sounds like the article's gone viral."

"There's a documentary coming out about him, too," Michael added.

"Wow! He's famous! And to think he took something of mine," she said, holding the top against her.

"You should have him autograph it," the man said.

"Or paw-ograph it," Savannah suggested, joining him in laughter. "By the way, I'm Savannah and this is my husband Michael."

The woman held out her hand. "We're Sidney and Glenn."

"Nice to meet you," Savannah said, shaking hands with both of them.

Michael also greeted them with a handshake. "Do you live here on the beach or are you visiting?" Michael asked.

Glenn said, "We're staying at her parents' beach house. We're having our engagement party down there this weekend."

"Cool," Savannah said. "…and congratulations."

The couple nodded and smiled.

"You said you're visiting, right?" Glenn asked.

"Yes, for a few weeks," Savannah said. "Just got here last night." She scanned the area with her eyes. "This is just beautiful."

"Nice to have an ocean in your backyard," Michael added.

"Sure is," Glenn said. He leaned forward and asked, "Now, you haven't seen an extra flip-flop around have you? Could your cat carry away something like that?"

Savannah gasped. "Oh my gosh!" She looked down at Glenn's feet. "Wait here," she said, dashing back to the house. She returned carrying a brown size-eleven flip-flop. "Is this one yours?"

Sidney and Glenn began laughing. She covered her mouth with her hands. "Oh my Gosh. That's yours, isn't it, honey?"

He took it in his hands and shook his head slowly. "Yup, that's mine, all right." He looked at the cat again. "He carried it all the way here in his mouth?"

"As far as we know, he did," Michael said. "I've never seen him with a knapsack over his shoulder or wearing saddlebags."

Everyone laughed out loud.

"You'd better come in and see if he has anything else of yours," Savannah suggested.

Sidney smiled and responded enthusiastically, "Okay! I'd love to meet Rags. Is he friendly?"

"Very," Savannah said, leading the couple inside. Upon entering the room, Sidney knelt down and began petting the large cat. Rags allowed the petting for just a moment, then he joined the others, who were investigating his latest array of treasures. Sidney followed the cat and everyone watched as he jumped up on the ottoman and sat next to the items.

"He sure looks proud of himself," Glenn said.

Savannah nodded. "Oh yes; he's a showoff."

"Now, what does he do, go back and forth carrying each of these things one at a time?" Glenn asked.

"I think so," Savannah said. "I don't know how else he'd get it all here, unless he has an accomplice," she said, giggling.

"Hey," Sidney said, pointing, "I wonder if that's the toy the old man next door was looking for. Said it was his dog's favorite. He left it out all night and it was gone this morning. He accused my little niece and nephew of taking it. But it was the cat, huh?"

Glenn began to laugh. "He cracks me up." He reached out and petted Rags. "Man, you're some macho cat to get that toy away from Brutus." He explained, exaggerating, "He's a big German-shepherd-pony mix."

"That was his specialty, when we lived in LA," Savannah said. "He loved taking toys from big dogs. Once, he managed to bring home one of those tug-of-war-rope toys, which I found out later belonged to a couple of pit bulls." She picked up the dog toy and handed it to Glenn. "Take it," she said. "See if it belongs to your neighbor's dog."

Sidney shook her head. "Nothing else looks familiar." She scratched Rags around the neck and said, "Thanks for giving the stuff back, boy."

After Savannah and Michael had accompanied the young couple outside and waved goodbye, Michael said, "I'm curious about something."

Savannah eased into a chair and took a bite of her sandwich. "What?"

"How did you know that was her top? There've probably been six-dozen people walk by just since we came out here. Did you size her up, or what?"

"Michael," she said, "you're not very observant."

"What, you want me to look at women?"

"Uh, well…"

"Really, how did you know it was hers?"

She shook her head and grinned at him. "It's elementary, my good man," she quipped. "It matches the bikini bottoms she's wearing. You didn't notice that?"

Michael shook his head. "I guess I didn't, but you're right."

"About what?"

"I need to pay more attention to women wearing bikinis."

Savannah slapped at her husband playfully. "Just you never mind." Suddenly she sat up straight and cocked her head. "Is that the doorbell? It's probably Mom," she said as she disappeared into the house.

"Hi Mom," she said, reaching out to hug her. "Oh, you're loaded down there. Here, let me help you." She picked up a suitcase and carried it inside. "Did you have any trouble finding the house?"

Gladys Jordan shook her head. "Not at all. My GPS did a good job." She looked around. "This is lovely. It's so big! My goodness, three of my house would fit inside this one." She glanced toward the large sliding glass doors leading to the deck and lamented, "And I don't have a beach view."

"Well, you have one here for as long as you want to stay with us," Savannah said.

Gladys smiled brightly and asked, "Okay, where's my beautiful granddaughter?"

"Napping," Savannah said. "Oh wait, she must be awake. Here comes Buffy."

Both women watched as the fluffy little cat trotted down the carpeted staircase toward them.

"What does that sweet cat have to do with Lilliana's nap time?" Gladys asked.

"Buffy watches over Lily when she's sleeping. When the baby wakes up, Buffy comes to tell us." Savannah chuckled. "I guess she doesn't know we have a perfectly good baby monitor."

"Well that's pretty unusual, isn't it?" Gladys asked.

"What can I tell you?" Savannah said. "We have some pretty unusual cats. Wait until you hear about Rags's latest escapade."

After Savannah changed Lily, she showed her mother to her room. "I thought we'd put you here, on the other side of the alcove where Lily sleeps."

"Oh, I love it," Gladys said. She shivered a little. "My very own ocean view—this is so nice!"

"You can have a larger room, but there's a mountain view," Savannah offered.

"No, I'd rather have this view. You know me and the ocean. I've always wanted to live at the beach. Only…"

"Only what?" Savannah asked.

She made a face. "Only, I'm not crazy about sand in the house."

Savannah smiled at her mom. "I imagine there's a whole lot of vacuuming and sweeping that goes on in these beach homes." She added," Michael and I are having a sandwich on the deck. I picked up an extra turkey and Swiss; want one?"

"That would be nice. Thank you," she said as they made their way down the stairs.

"Here," Savannah said, handing the baby to Gladys. "Go on out and join Michael on the deck. I'll get you and Lily some lunch. Is iced tea okay?"

"Sounds great," Gladys said, smothering Lily's head with kisses. "Come on, you little cherub. Let's go see what Daddy's doing."

*** 

"Hi, you two," Peter said when he saw Savannah and Michael enter the patio at Rudy's Beachfront Bistro around seven that evening. "Sorry I wasn't at the gallery to meet you. Something came up."

"That's okay. We found the place just fine," Savannah said.

As they sat down at Peter's table, Michael asked, "No date tonight?"

Peter shook his head. "Not tonight." He motioned for the server. "What do you want to drink?" he asked his tablemates.

"Light beer," Savannah said.

Michael nodded.

"Make it three," Peter told the waitress.

After the server had walked away, Michael pulled something out of his pocket and handed it to Peter. "What's with the artwork on the note you left us at the gallery?"

"What?" Peter asked, lowering his brows. He opened the note and read, "Meet me at Rudy's." Peter had drawn an arrow pointing to the right. Under that, in bold, black ink was a skull and crossbones. "What the…?" Peter said. "That's not my art. I wonder who…" he started, then he shook his head. "Probably just someone with nothing better to do…a beach bum, maybe. No, I didn't draw the skull." He crumpled the note in his palm. "Sorry about that."

"No problem," Michael said. "I didn't take it seriously. Just figured you were joking around." When Peter didn't respond, Michael asked, "So, Peter, is this the sort of thing you're dealing with? Is this why you want the cameras installed?"

He nodded. "Yup."

"Well, let's set a time when I can take a look around the gallery."

"Ah, the brewkis are here. I'm thirsty," Peter said. He smiled up at the young server. "Thank you, honey. Just in the nick of time." He took a swig and then looked across the table at Michael. In a more serious tone, he said, "Yeah, maybe before-hours one day."

After a few moments of silence, Michael said, "Hey, Peter, to finish a conversation we…or I…started earlier…a conversation you expertly ducked," he said, smirking, "…did you ever marry?"

Peter pursed his lips. He took in a deep breath, glanced around the room, and then leaned toward Michael. "Here's the deal, Michael, I'm…"

Michael pulled back from the table, eyebrows raised. "You're not going to say you're…"

Savannah saw the couple at the next table glance up from their intimate conversation when they heard Peter's thunderous laughter. Peter shook his head. "No, I'm not gay. That's Roger. Remember Roger?"

"Yeah, I remember Roger. Gay?" Michael asked, disbelieving.

"As a happy Girl Scout," Peter said, nodding. He took a deep breath before continuing. "No, I never married. Don't have any kids. The most recent love of my life—in female form—walked out last month. She was everything I wanted. But she didn't want any part of the competition."

Michael looked puzzled. "Competition?"

"His art," Savannah said. "Your first love, right, Peter?"

Peter nodded. "You got it, smart lady."

"Oh," Michael said, "so your biggest asset in attracting women is also your biggest detriment?"

Peter chuckled. "You might say that." He shook his head. "Yeah, I can get 'em. I just can't seem to keep 'em."

"Why not date another artist?" Michael suggested, obviously pleased with his grand idea. "…someone who understands the artist's rather…eccentric ways?"

"Michael," Savannah said, setting down her glass. She grinned at him. "Two artists? That's absurd."

"Why?" he asked. He looked from one to the other of his tablemates.

"Yeah, why?" Peter asked, appearing equally clueless.

"I just can't imagine two serious artists together, that's all." When the two men continued to stare at her, she explained, "Well, artists are…talented. As Peter alluded to, they're competitive and, frankly, those I've met—present company excepted, of course—they tend to be a bit flakey."

"Flakey?" Michael repeated. "Savannah, that wasn't…"

"Wait a minute, Michael," Peter said, "she speaks the truth. I've never had a successful relationship or even a long-term one with another good artist. And the breakups—they're the worst," he said, grimacing. "Oh no…she's right. Women artists are flakey and they have fragile psyches. I dated one who criticized every stroke I put on canvas." He smiled. "Oh, she loved the way I stroked her…" He turned serious again. "…but when it came to my art, she was the most severe and unfair critic I've ever encountered. It was emasculating," he said. "I almost lost my will to paint. I even started seeing a shrink." He winked. "…dated her for a while, too."

Michael grinned. "How did that end?"

"Not bad. I actually accepted some of her…ahem… non-professional advice and took a flying leap—out of that debacle. That's when I established new rules for myself: Don't date artists, your shrink, or your attorney."

Michael shook his head. "You dated your attorney? You scoundrel. What did that cost you?"

Peter looked sheepish. "Never mind. I now have a male attorney."

"So, outside of your…can I even call it a love life…?" Michael said, chuckling. "…what is the problem you spoke of? Is that related to women?"

"Good gosh, I hope not," Peter said.

"So what's going on, may we ask?" Michael persisted.

"Hard to explain. Near misses, communication glitches, innuendoes…" He picked up the wadded note and said, "…intrusions like this. It's like someone's trying to rattle me—distract me from my work." He rested both elbows on the table in front of him and said, "…or maybe hurt me; I'm not sure."

"So it's things like this showing up at your home that has your housekeeper frightened?" Savannah asked.

Peter pursed his lips. He nodded and went on, "Nothing dangerous…yet…but unnerving, nonetheless."

"Has this always been the case?" Savannah asked.

"Oh no," he said. "I've been painting for the last thirteen years. I came out of the closet with my art in 2003

and my work really began to take off five years ago. All was
hunky-dory until… well, about a month ago, I'd say. Little
things started happening. Little things like this…" he said,
referring to the note, "but also some more serious attacks. A
bad review—actually downright slander—missing paintings,
problems with bookings and show arrangements…it's all
very mysterious and unsettling."

"It seems to have you a little shaken," Michael said.

"To tell you the truth…" he started.

"Hi Peter."

The trio looked up and saw an attractive woman of
about forty-five standing next to their table. "Hi Dawna,"
Peter said, rising to greet her. He brushed his fashionably
unshaven cheek briefly against her flawless one. "How's it
going?" he asked.

"Good," she said, glancing across the table at the
Iveys.

Peter cleared his throat and addressed his guests.
"Uh, this is my right—and left—hand, Dawna—with a W,"
he added, as if it were important to do so. "Dawna, this is my
long-time friend Michael and his wife Savannah."

The woman smiled and nodded in greeting, the
auburn highlights in her hair shining in the soft twinkle lights
that were casually strung around the patio dining area.

Savannah and Michael acknowledged her, as well.

"Have you eaten, Dawna?" Peter asked. When she
shook her head, he reached toward a nearby table and pulled
another chair over, inviting her to join them, saying, "Here,
sit with us. We're just about to order."

"Thanks," she said, easing her shapely body into
the chair across from Savannah. "I hate eating alone." She
grinned at Savannah and Michael. "That's why I come in
here. I always see someone I know."

48

"So you work for this starving artist?" Michael asked, playfully.

Dawna nodded.

"She manages the gallery, schedules my shows, does the shipping, PR…you name it," Peter said. "Without Dawna, my life would be…well, more of a mess than it is." He leaned in as if telling a secret. "At least my professional life is in good order," he said, winking.

Michael grinned. "You must be some woman to keep this guy in line."

Dawna glanced at Michael and then Peter, saying, "He's not an easy man to organize."

Savannah eyed the woman as she bantered with the men. When there was an opening, she asked, "Dawna, how did you become involved in this field—I mean as manager of a gallery? Is it the art that attracted you or the business aspect?"

The woman narrowed her dark-blue eyes as if in contemplation and answered, "Both, actually. I was an art major…many years ago. But when I realized there were only a chosen few who would make it in this field, I decided I'd better use my brain instead of my heart and I went back to school to learn the business side of the art world."

Savannah smiled. "How resourceful of you."

"Yeah, flexible," Michael said.

"So do you miss your art?" Savannah asked.

Dawna looked around the room and then glanced briefly at Savannah. She smiled weakly and said, "No, I don't have time for that. I'm so embedded in Peter's that there's no time to pursue my own." She cocked her head, her long hair flowing across her low-cut neckline. "Keeping Peter in the limelight is my passion now."

"You've sure done a nice job of exhibiting Peter's paintings at the gallery," Michael said.

"Oh, you've visited the gallery?" she asked.

Michael nodded.

Before he could comment, Savannah said, "As far as I can tell, it's the best one in the little shopping district."

"The best one in the state," Dawna said, smiling.

Peter grinned at Dawna. "Thanks to this dynamo. She keeps my name and my art in front of the public."

"We saw all of those articles about Peter," Michael said. "So you run the gallery and do the promotion, too?" he asked.

Dawna nodded.

"I keep offering to get her some help. Heck, she didn't even want me to hire Kara," Peter explained. He looked at Dawna. "But I think she has taken some of the pressure off, hasn't she?"

Dawna started to respond when the waitress approached the table, prepared to take their orders. When she left, Savannah addressed Dawna: "I'm curious."

"About what?" Dawna asked.

"About why you wouldn't want help with all that you do?"

Dawna appeared to be uncomfortable. She squirmed in her seat, rearranged her silverware, took in a deep breath, and finally said, "I just don't need it, that's all. I've got it covered." She looked at Peter. "I know what he needs sometimes better than he does and I know how to make things happen."

Savannah smiled. "Sounds like he's lucky to have you."

Michael leaned forward, his elbows on the table in front of him. "So Peter, you started to tell us about what has you…"

Peter quickly interrupted, saying, "What has me so nervous? It's the show Saturday night." He began speaking more loudly and quickly. "It's a charity thing. I just hope we can make a good showing for their project. As I understand it, the proceeds go toward art programs in local schools. Dawna set it up, didn't you?" he asked, acknowledging her.

She nodded. "It'll give Peter exposure among those celebrities who don't already know about him, as well."

"Right. It'll be a fun evening." He winked at Savannah. "Bring your autograph book." When he noticed the waitress heading in their direction carrying a platter, Peter leaned back in his chair and said, "Here come our appetizers."

Savannah looked intently at Peter. *What was that all about?"* she wondered. *He sure got worked up and excited there all of a sudden.* She looked at Michael, who didn't seem to notice, as he was busy buttering a piece of French bread.

When the two couples had finished eating, Peter asked, "Dawna, are you going to the concert?"

She shook her head. "No. I have some things I need to do." She gathered up her purse and sweater, saying, "Nice to meet you two. Enjoy your stay at the beach."

Peter picked up his credit card and put it in his wallet. "Well, let's get out of here, shall we?"

Once on the street, Michael nudged Peter and said, "Man, you sure know how to pick employees. She's attractive."

Peter laughed. "Yeah, I do, don't I? I like pretty things around me. What can I say?" He glanced at Savannah. "…and it's a good thing you have a beautiful wife or I might have kicked you out of my beach house by now."

Savannah grinned and shook her head. "I never thought I'd meet a playboy artist," she said.

"Playboy artist," Peter said, as if in contemplation. "Hey, that's a good title for my memoirs, don't you think?"

"You're too much," Michael said, slapping Peter on the back.

Just then Savannah noticed something. *That's Dawna,* she thought to herself, when she spotted a woman across the street standing in the shadows between two buildings. *That looks like the black-and-white dress she was wearing.* Savannah slowed her pace and strained to see what she was doing. *Looks like she's arguing with someone. She doesn't look happy.* In a brief few seconds, Dawna stepped out onto the pavement and walked away at a fast pace. That's when Savannah spotted a man hurrying off in the opposite direction. *Hey, that's the guy I saw earlier at the gallery window. I wonder why she was talking to him. Maybe he asked her for a handout. She must have given him something. He looks happy.*

Savannah heard Michael calling to her. "Hey, you're dawdling."

She hastened her pace to catch up. "It's so balmy," she commented, as they walked into a park where a half-dozen musicians were setting up in a large gazebo. "Do you ever have to drive anywhere?" she asked. "Everything seems to be within walking distance."

"We bicycle a lot and, yes, walk. That's how it is in a beach community; casual. Want to sit here?" Peter asked, motioning toward a grassy knoll overlooking the informal stage.

"Sure," Michael said. "Okay, Savannah?"

"Fine with me," she agreed. "The grass isn't wet, is it?"

"No, I don't think so." Peter knelt down and felt it.

"Hi Peter." Everyone turned and saw Kara walking toward them carrying a large blanket folded over one arm. She smiled at Michael and Savannah, who nodded in greeting.

"Hi, Kara," Peter said. "Are you with anyone," he asked, looking around.

"No," she said, shyly. "But I have a blanket to share."

"Cool. Want to sit here?" Peter asked.

"Sure," she said, handing him the blanket.

Once Peter and Kara had spread the blanket, he sat down and invited the others to join him. Kara lowered herself easily next to Peter; Savannah and Michael plopped down in front of them on the shallow slope. While the musicians tuned their instruments, the two couples discussed their music preferences and performances they'd attended. When she had the opportunity, Savannah asked Kara, "Did Peter say you're a college student?"

"Yes, I attend the art institute."

"What kind of art are you interested in?" she asked.

She chuckled. "I'm fickle. I keep changing my mind. I hope I can settle down to one medium and one style eventually. Right now, I just want to create." She glanced at Peter. "I haven't found my niche, yet. Every time they introduce a subject and a medium at school, that becomes my favorite," she said, laughing.

"I don't think you're fickle," Michael said. "You're just diverse—and you must be multi-talented."

She winced a little. "I didn't say I was good at everything I try."

"But how cool that you're willing to expand your horizons," Savannah said. "I hope our children will try everything that interests them—well, within reason. Then when they choose their path, it's more likely to be a good fit. If they don't try it, they'll never know if they'd like it or not."

"Good philosophy," Peter said. "Is that how you chose your path?"

Savannah laughed. "Of course not. I liked animals and science growing up and I became a veterinarian. End of story." She looked at Michael. "…well, then I got sidetracked." She wrapped one arm around Michael's neck and kissed him on the cheek. "Sure glad I took that fork in the road," she said, laughing.

"And you, Michael," Kara asked, "have you taken any detours?"

Michael thought for a moment and said, "Professionally, no, but I did try something once that didn't work out. In the end, there were rewards greater than I could ever imagine."

"Are you talking about your disappointing marriage and later finding out you had a son?" Peter asked.

Michael nodded.

"We learned about his son on the eve of our wedding day," Savannah explained. "Can you imagine?"

"And you married him, anyway?" Peter asked.

"Oh, yes and I'm so glad I did. Adam is a wonderful, bright child. We love him very much," she said.

Michael grinned at her and added, "He's coming here tomorrow. We have all sorts of plans."

"A trip to Disneyland?" Peter asked.

Michael lowered his brows. "Uh…well…not sure about that…"

Peter ran one hand over his whisker stubble and said, "Been wanting a day of play. How about I chauffer your family to the Magic Kingdom?"

Savannah and Michael exchanged looks. Michael's eyes widened. "That might be fun. We could all go."

"Not me," Kara said. "I'll be working."

"I'll have a talk with that boss of yours," Michael joked. "Sounds like a real slave-driver."

Kara studied Peter's face. "Oh, he takes pretty good care of me," she said, smiling.

Once the orchestra started to play, the two couples rested comfortably on the blanket and enjoyed the music. After several minutes, Savannah noticed Kara texting on her phone. "Charlynn's here," she told Peter, quietly. She looked out over the crowd and then raised one hand and began waving at someone. Savannah saw a hand go up in the midst of a group. Kara smiled and did more texting. "She's going to take my place at the gallery for a few days next week, okay?" she asked Peter.

He shrugged. "Whatever you two work out is fine with me." He looked at her. "Going somewhere exciting?"

"Just a couple of days in Catalina with friends."

"Sounds fun."

The concert ended at nine-thirty, but the small crowd continued milling around the area for a while longer. That's when Kara called out, "Hi Char."

Just then, Charlynn walked toward the group. Peter greeted her warmly and introduced her to his guests.

"Oh, the folks from north of us," Charlynn said. "Nice to meet you. Are you enjoying your stay?"

Michael nodded and Savannah said, "Very much, so far. Just got here yesterday."

"How'd you like our little concert?"

"Seems to be quite an accomplished group of musicians," Michael said.

"Yes. Most of them have been playing together for years." She turned and pointed. "The base player's my uncle. He retired from some big orchestra in New York a few years ago and now plays here for fun."

"Cool," Savannah said.

Just then, Charlynn stood on her tiptoes and waved to a young man sitting on an idling motorized scooter. "Oh, there's my ride," she said. "Better go." She hugged Kara and then Peter and scurried into the milling crowd.

"Are you going out somewhere?" Kara asked, as Peter and Michael folded her blanket and handed it to her.

Peter shook his head. "No, we have to go in early tomorrow, remember? I'm getting ready for that show." He hugged her, gave her a quick kiss on the cheek, and said, "Now, you go get some rest, will ya?"

The trio watched Kara walk away, but Savannah was the only one who noticed what happened next. *That man,* she thought, *he's the one I saw at the gallery this morning and earlier with Dawna. Did he just speak to Kara as she walked past him? Who is he? What is his connection to these women?*

"Coming?" Michael called, as he noticed Savannah lagging behind again.

"I could use a cup of coffee or a nightcap; are you two game or do you have to get back?" Peter asked when Savannah had caught up.

Michael and Savannah looked at each other. He said, "Hey, we're on vacation. You're the one who has to get up early."

Peter shrugged. "Yeah, I had to tell Kara something or she'd be coming home with me again."

Savannah raised her eyebrows. "Oh?"

Michael slapped Peter on the back. "You dog, you. A college student? How old is she?"

"Older than she looks," Peter said, winking.

"Well, she is cute," Michael said, "isn't she, hon?"

"Sure is. You have good taste in…uh…employees," Savannah said. "I enjoyed meeting Charlynn, too. So she works in the gallery, as well?"

"Yes. She and Kara are friends from school and they swap jobs sometimes. Kara can do the framing and Charlynn can pinch-hit as a hostess at the gallery. Interchangeable," he said, smiling. He stopped in front of a coffee house. "Let's get some java. I want to talk to you some more."

Once they had picked up their orders—three coffees and three bowls of gelato—and found a table, Michael said, "There's something I'm curious about."

"What's that?" Peter asked.

"You say Dawna is your right hand in your business, yet you seemed reluctant to discuss with her the stuff that's been going on. What's up with that?"

Peter leaned toward Michael and lowered his voice. "Hey, I trust that woman with my life, but my PI says I can't make myself vulnerable that way right now—especially with people close to me." He sighed. "I'm going crazy here. I feel like a heel not coming clean with Dawna and the others. Hell, they could be in danger, so it doesn't seem right to keep them in the dark. But that's one reason I got in touch with you, Michael." He thinned his lips, looked Michael in the eyes, and said, "I need a friend." He looked sullen. "I just don't know who my friends are, anymore."

"But you said there's art missing. Dawna must know about that," Savannah reasoned.

"Sure, she knows about that and the booking snafus. But I haven't told her about all the incidents of harassment and vandalism or that I suspect it could be sabotage. According to Blake, I have to consider everyone around me a suspect until we figure out what's going on." He sipped his coffee. "You see, it's all hitting so close to home; it could be someone in my tight circle of employees or friends. Blake even wants me to keep Mama Maria in the dark."

"So that's why you started with the double-talk at dinner, huh?" Savannah said.

Peter nodded.

"You've hired a private eye?" Michael asked.

"Yes," Peter said. "Elizabeth Blake Eastman. Maybe you've heard of her. She took over her dad's agency. She also writes murder mysteries."

Michael smirked. "And where is she, beauty-wise, on a scale of one to ten?"

Peter smiled, sheepishly. He edged his cell out of his pocket, pulled up a website, and handed the phone to Michael. "See for yourself."

"Wow!" Michael held the phone toward Savannah.

"Ooh, exotic-looking. Is she East Indian?" she asked.

"I think her mother's from Sri Lanka," he said.

58

Michael handed the phone back to Peter, shaking his head.

"Charlynn's cute, too. She looks a lot like a friend of mine," Savannah said. "I think Bonnie is half or three-quarters black. Charlynn is taller than my friend, though. Bonnie's real petite."

"But none of your…ladies know about the behind-the-scenes stuff?" Michael asked.

Peter shook his head. "Not really. Mama Maria has had a few scares—she found a threatening note. There were a few incidents of graffiti. No. Blake wants me to keep it to myself for now. As I said, Dawna is closest to the operation of the gallery and my corporation—Peter Whitcomb Art. She knows we've had some problems, but she isn't privy to everything that goes on. She doesn't know I hired a PI, for example."

Michael grinned at his friend. "You and your Peter's Angels." He then asked, "About the cameras—you want them hidden, then, right?"

"Yes. I want to keep an eye on what's going on inside my studio and the gallery."

"How many people have access to your studio?" Savannah asked. "Seems like that's pretty private, isn't it?"

Peter sighed. "Well, we have meetings at my place sometimes and we had a celebration there a few weeks ago. It was after that shindig that I found one of my paintings all slashed up and stashed behind some framed prints. All of my employees were there, but so were a lot of other people. It could have happened that night, although I didn't find the vandalism until several days later."

Michael locked eyes with his friend. "Peter, just what do you hope to achieve or learn from these cameras?"

"Who's playing dirty with me. Who's trying to ruin my business. Who wants to hurt me."

Michael ran his hand through his straight brown hair and said, "Well, the way you have the gallery designed, I don't think cameras will be very effective. In order to see every corner and hidey-hole, you'd need so many cameras, it would be rather ridiculous. Now, if you were to open the area up, you'd be able to use one or two cameras in the main gallery, maybe one in the backroom…do you want one in your office?" he asked.

"Yes, definitely in the office. In fact, it's more important to have cameras in the office than out in the gallery," Peter explained.

Michael nodded. "Yeah, I could put one or two up in your gallery office and that backroom, as well as in your studio at home. Would that give you the coverage you need?"

Peter thought for a moment and said, "Yes, and how about just one in the main gallery, say, aimed toward the front door?"

"We could do that. It would mean cutting into the walls, unless there's some other way we could camouflage small cameras—behind your art or inside statues, for example."

"What kind of tools do you think you'll need?" Peter asked.

"Probably a screwdriver, a small drill, maybe a saw, pliers…" Michael said.

"There might be tools at the beach house. Dad used to piddle."

Michael looked puzzled. "Piddle?"

"Yeah, you know, fix things—make things…."

Savannah started laughing. "Piddle? So that's what you've been doing around our house, huh, Michael—piddling?"

Michael sat unsmiling. Finally he said, "Well, if I piddle, then I guess Peter doodles."

Savannah and Peter looked at Michael, glanced at each other, and then burst out laughing. Michael soon joined them in the laughter.

"Guess we struck a chord with him," Peter said.

"Yes," she said between chortles, "a sour one."

Peter squeezed Michael's shoulder playfully, "Hey, let's continue this discussion later." He yawned. "I'm ready to turn in, how about you two?"

***

"What an amazing day," Michael said, jumping out of bed and throwing open the curtains.

"Ouch," Savannah said, rolling over. "All that sunshine's hurting my eyes."

"There's no morning sunshine on this side of the house, hon."

"Well, it's bright!" she complained.

He walked into the alcove where Lily slept and promptly returned. "I guess your mother beat us to her, this morning." He chuckled. "She probably waited outside the door for her to wake up."

"Or she woke her up," Savannah said, yawning.

Michael laid down on the bed next to Savannah and enveloped her in his arms. "So what do you want for breakfast?" he mumbled into her neck.

"Are you cooking this morning?"

"Sure, if you don't mind cold cereal and canned

applesauce. We really need to go to the grocery store."
Michael propped himself up on one elbow and ran his fingers
along Savannah's shoulder. "You know who's coming
today," he said in a sing-song fashion.

Savannah smiled. "Adam. What big plans do you
guys have?"

"Well, they'll arrive late this afternoon, so I'm
thinking we'll hit the beach—maybe have a wiener and
marshmallow roast this evening. What do you think? Little
Rose would enjoy that, too."

"I'm sure she will." She snuggled closer to Michael.
"Well, we'd better go get that cold cereal. We have a big day
ahead."

Fifteen minutes later, Savannah and Michael entered
the kitchen. "Hi sweetie," Savannah said, rushing to Lily and
lifting her out of her chair. She held her close and murmured,
"I missed my girl." She looked at Gladys. "How'd it go last
night, Mom? Everything okay?"

"Oh yes. We had a great time. How did you get
such an agreeable baby, Vannie?" she asked. "You were a
handful."

"I was?" Savannah asked, frowning. "You never told
me that. I thought Bri was the challenging child."

"Yes, as a teen, but you were the fussy baby.
Nothing suited you. Of course, you were my first and I was
inexperienced, so maybe my expectations were unrealistic."

Just then, Savannah thought she heard something.
"Was that the doorbell?"

"Yeah," Michael said heading toward the living
room. "I'll get it."

Savannah joined him at the front door and was
stunned to see Sidney standing on the porch. Glenn stood

next to her, holding Rags in his arms. "Oh my gosh," she said. "Where did you find him?"

The couple chuckled and Sidney said, "He was out on our deck."

Michael grimaced. "He returned to the scene of the crime, did he?"

"Yes, and he had something with him," Glenn said, opening his hand to reveal a dollar bill.

"Oh Rags," Savannah scolded.

Michael took the cat, saying to him, "You know, you could do hard time for stealing money, buddy."

"Gosh, thank you so much for bringing him back," Savannah said. She cringed. "I hope he didn't disturb any of your stuff."

"Oh no," Sidney said, smiling. "We enjoyed his visit. Not a problem."

"Mom!" Savannah called once the couple had left. "Did you let Rags out? A neighbor just brought him home."

Gladys looked up at her daughter. "I don't think so." She thought about it and said, "I did walk out on the deck with the baby earlier to let her watch the birds, maybe he slipped out then. I'm sorry. He's okay, isn't he?"

"Yes, he's fine."

"Good. Now dear, would you two like your juice and coffee on the deck this morning?"

Savannah thought about it and said, "That would be lovely, Mom. Let's do that."

"You go get situated out there with the baby and I'll bring it out. Go on, now," Gladys encouraged, waving her hand in that direction. Michael picked up the baby chair and headed for the deck. Savannah followed him with Lily in her arms.

Suddenly Savannah said, "Is that your phone, hon?"

He listened. "Oh yeah," he said, walking into the kitchen where he'd left it.

Before he returned to the deck, Gladys appeared carrying a tray. "You both take your coffee black, right?"

"Yup," Savannah said. "Thanks. How nice. It's a pretty morning, isn't it?"

"Sure is," Gladys said, sitting down in a deck chair and picking up a cup of coffee.

"We're going to have more company," Michael announced upon joining the women on the deck.

Savannah set her coffee cup down. "Oh, who?"

"Peter," he said, appearing rather puzzled.

"Do you mean for breakfast?" Savannah asked.

"No. He said he needs to leave his studio and wants to move over here. I didn't notice it, but there's a loft above the garage. He keeps it locked—off-limits to renters. He says he needs to move in there for at least a couple of days. He'll bring the dog. A neighbor will take care of the cats."

"Sure, it's his house. I don't have a problem with it, do you, Michael?"

"No, I guess not. Like you said, it's his house. I invited him to the wiener roast tonight."

"Well, I don't see how you could not invite him. That's fine," she said. She reached down and petted Lexie as she walked past. "You're going to have a friend come visit, Lexie. You'll have a doggie pal to romp with on the beach."

***

"You're quite the boogie-boarder, Son," Michael said, tousling the boy's hair as they walked from the beach toward the deck with Adam's stepfather late that afternoon.

"Yeah, he's athletic. Loves the water," Eric said.

"Looks like you know your way around the water, too, Eric."

"Yeah, I was a surfer in my younger days. I still enjoy the thrill of it, just don't get to do it as often as I'd like."

"I know how that goes—priorities change when you start building a family," Michael said.

Eric nodded. "You got that right."

"Hey, you looked good out there," Savannah said to Adam as they stepped up on the deck.

"He's my little shark," Marci said, smiling.

"Hi ya'll," Peter said, joining the others. "Been swimming?" he asked Adam when he saw the three of them walk up.

Adam nodded. "I rode my boogie board a long ways, didn't I, Dad?"

"He sure did," Michael said. "He must have skimmed fifteen or twenty feet on that one run."

"Really?" Peter said, his eyes widening.

The boy smiled from ear to ear. "Yeah, it was a long one."

"You must be Adam," Peter said.

Michael smoothed his wet hair back with one hand. "Oh, I'm sorry. Yes, this is Adam, my son. And this is Eric." He addressed Eric, "Peter owns this great house."

"You do?" Adam said, excitedly. "I'd sure like to have a beach in my yard."

Eric grabbed the boy playfully around the back of the neck. "And a horse, and a skateboard park, and…"

Adam grinned up at his stepdad.

"Did you meet Marci and their daughter Rose?" Michael asked as they walked toward where the women sat in deck chairs.

"Hello," Peter said, bowing slightly. He reached down and touched Rose's head as the three-year-old played with a toy.

"Ready for a wiener roast?" Michael asked. "Sun's almost down. Us guys worked up an appetite. Anyone else hungry?"

"Sure are," Savannah said. "Marci and I were about to dig into those stale donuts in there."

Marci laughed, "Not!"

An hour and a half later, after everyone had eaten their quota of hot dogs and Gladys's famous smashed potato salad, the doorbell rang. Michael answered it. When he returned, he wasn't alone. "Someone to see you, Peter," he announced.

Peter seemed stunned to see Dawna standing there with Michael. She briefly acknowledged Savannah and then asked Peter if they could talk in private. He hesitated, set his beer bottle on a nearby table, and led her into the living room.

Fifteen minutes later, Savannah walked through the living room toward the staircase on her way to put the baby to bed. She acknowledged the couple, who seemed to be engaged in a serious conversation. *Wow,* she thought, *Peter's body language is telling. He's not pleased with whatever message Dawna has brought. Poor guy.*

It was on Savannah's return trip toward the living room, baby monitor in hand, that she caught a glimpse of Rags racing past her. *Did he have something in his mouth?* she wondered. She followed the cat back up the stairs into Gladys's room and coaxed him to let her look at his latest treasure. *A business card.* "Where did you get this, Rags?" she asked as she examined it. She reached out and petted the cat. "I'm sorry, buddy," she told him, "I really do have to find out if this is important to anyone. If no one wants it, it's yours. How about that?" She laughed softly, thinking, *Gosh, here I am negotiating with a cat.*

Savannah looked at the card. *"Peter Whitcomb Art Gallery. Kara Little, Hostess." Darn thieving cat,* she thought. She turned the card over. *Hmm, someone wrote a note on the back. Gads, it's hard to read—really tiny and scribbley. "Job done. Want $100 NOW. Meet side Joe's 8" This is embarrassing,* she thought. *Where did this come from? Kara hasn't been here—unless she's been to Peter's loft above the garage. But how would Rags find his way there?*

She sprinted easily down the stairs and into the living room, where she approached Peter and Dawna. "I'm sorry to interrupt," she said, grimacing. She held out the card toward Peter and turned it over once. "I found Kara's card..."

Dawna took one look at it and quickly grabbed it, burying it in her hand. "Where'd you get this?" she almost demanded, glancing down at her purse and back up at Savannah.

"Oh, sorry. I thought it was Kara's."

"Well, yeah...it is..." she stammered. "I...um..." She scrutinized Savannah, her eyes narrowed. "Where did you find it?"

"The cat steals things," she explained.

"Cat?" Dawna said. "I didn't see a cat, did you, Peter?"

"Um..."

"He can be sneaky," Savannah said. "I apologize."

Dawna seemed to glare at Savannah for a moment, then her demeanor softened. "No harm done," she said, picking up her purse and shoving the card into one of the pockets. As Savannah started to walk away, Dawna said, "I'll make sure Kara gets it back." She then stood. "Well, Peter, let's continue this tomorrow, shall we?"

"Sure," he said, walking with her to the front door. Dawna had stepped out and was headed for her car when Peter called, "Wait. That won't work. I'm taking the day off tomorrow."

Dawna turned and looked at him. "Oh? Going out of town?"

"Yes, as a matter of fact—to Disneyland with the Iveys," he said, smiling.

"Okay. That'll be…good…I mean, everything will be fine." She seemed to get a new burst of energy, saying, "I have to go; lots to do," as she sprinted off to her car.

***

Friday morning after Adam's mother, stepfather, and sister had left for home, the entire household of vacationers piled into the Iveys' SUV and headed to Disneyland with Peter as their guide.

"How long since you've been to Disneyland, Peter?" Savannah asked from the middle seat, where she sat with her mother.

He laughed. "Gosh, since I was a kid, I guess."

"I'm excited to enjoy it with my grandchildren," Gladys said. She then spoke up a little. "Have you been there before, Adam?" she asked. After a few moments, she craned her neck to look at him, and asked again, "Have you been to Disneyland before?"

He said, "Yes, Grandma Jordan. I nodded to you."

Savannah looked back at the boy and smiled. "When someone's not looking at you, you have to respond using words," she said. "They can't see a nod when they're not looking."

"Oh, sorry," he said, quietly. He explained, "I went to Disneyland once when I was a baby, but I don't remember it."

"Then you're in for a treat," Gladys said. "Have you been before, Grandma Jordan?" he asked.

"Sure have. I took Savannah and Brianna when they were about your age. I went again a few years ago with one of my sisters and her grandchildren. It's really an awesome place." She turned to Savannah. "Will the animals be okay while we're gone all day?"

"Well, this is Peter's cleaning lady's day at the beach house. She'll check on things and let the dogs out," Savannah assured her. "I just hope Rags doesn't bamboozle her into letting him out, that juvenile cat-linquent."

"Cat-linquent?" Adam asked. "What's that?"

"It's a play on the words *cat* and *delinquent*," Savannah explained.

"Oh," Adam said, "a made-up word."

She nodded. "That's right."

In the front seat, Michael and Peter were discussing world issues, their chosen professions, and finally the topic came around to Peter's current predicament. "So Peter, can you tell me what happened to make you move out of your place on the hill?" He punched his friend in the shoulder. "Get tired of that walk?"

"Naw, just missed you guys. Wanted to be part of the family fun," he said, smiling. He became somber. "It's been a while since I've enjoyed family life. You know, my parents both died in a small plane crash five years ago."

"No, I didn't know. That must have been a shock."

"Yes, I miss them. Dad and I did a lot of things together—he was still quite athletic." He turned to Michael. "You lost both of your parents, too, didn't you?"

"Yes, Mom died of cancer when I was still in veterinary school."

Peter nodded, unsmiling. "I remember that. She was so young."

"Yes, and Dad…well, I wouldn't be surprised if it was suicide. He never recovered after we lost Mom. He died in a freak one-car accident the following year. They say he was drinking, but I never knew my dad to overdo it with anything—drinking, gambling, eating, speeding…"

Peter glanced toward the backseat, where Gladys and Savannah chatted. "She's the lucky one," he said, motioning toward Savannah. "And so is your baby daughter."

"I'm the lucky one," Michael said. "I couldn't be happier." In a more serious tone, he asked, "So, what really caused you to leave your place, Peter?"

Peter spoke more softly now:  "My PI advised it—said she sensed I was in danger there."

Michael let out a sigh and shook his head. "Women run your life, man,"

"Yes; and your point is?" he asked, grinning.

"She senses something?" Michael asked. "Is she a psychic PI?"

Peter shrugged. "Naw, just intuitive, I guess."

"Really?"

"Yeah, she's a fascinating gal. Seems to have a pipeline to the underground—whatever that consists of in the art world—and she sorta follows her gut feelings. She told me I didn't have to move, but she strongly advised it. She said something about negative energy."

"Wow," Michael said. "That's crazy stuff, coming from a PI." He glanced at Peter a couple of times. "And you buy into it?"

"Well, I'm paying her. Might as well do what she says." He shifted in his seat so he faced Michael. "She's sure been right-on with her…ideas…so far. And I had a wonderful night's sleep for a change."

Michael was quiet for a few miles and then asked, shooting a glance into the rearview mirror to make sure the women were still occupied in their conversation, "So which ones are you dating?"

Peter eyed Michael solemnly. "None of them, as far as I'm concerned. But…"

"But what?" Michael asked, grinning.

"Well, I think some of those women believe there's more to our…partnerships…than just professional. I guess I somehow give off vibes that I don't mean to. Kara's too young, Charlynn's a bit flighty. Dawna's just not my type." He sat with his thoughts for a moment before saying, "I've actually tried to fall for Dawna, but can't get beyond friendship."

"And Blake? What about her?" Michael asked.

"I wouldn't mind…" he started.

"Hey Dad," Adam called from the backseat. "Grandma says there's a pirate ship at Disneyland. Will you go on it with me?"

"Sure, Son," Michael said.

"You're probably tall enough to go on most of the rides," Peter told Adam.

"They measure you?" Adam asked.

"Yes, for some of the rides," Peter explained.

"Lily's probably too short to go on the rides, isn't she?" Adam asked.

Michael chuckled. "I think her only Disneyland ride will be in the stroller."

***

"Well, what a day," Michael said as he drove the family home that evening. "Did everyone have a good time?"

When there was no response, Michael said, "Hello, anyone back there?"

Savannah laughed quietly. "The backseat kids are sawing wood. Mom and I are about to fall asleep."

"That was great," Gladys said. "I don't know when I've had so much fun. Thank you for including me."

"Well, thank you for helping out with the kids," Michael said.

Gladys nodded. "You need a lot of eyes to keep track of them at a theme park."

"I had fun watching them have fun," Michael said. "Even Lily loved all the sights and sounds."

"She's sure cute," Peter said. "What a cool baby."

"We think so," Michael agreed.

"I'm using that picture I took of her in those Minnie Mouse ears as my phone screen photo."

Michael grinned at Peter. "So she's a pin-up girl already, huh? Next you'll want to paint her portrait."

Peter was quiet. "Not a bad idea, actually. She'd be a great subject. Her and your cat."

"Buffy?" Michael asked.

"Yeah, she's pretty, but I was thinking more about the regal one—Rags."

Savannah reached up and patted Michael on the shoulder. "You must be exhausted. I think Adam took you on every ride at the park."

"Yeah, I did things I never thought I'd do as an adult," he said. He tuned into his own thoughts for a moment before saying, "It's interesting how, when you have children, you revert back to your own childhood. In fact, today I did things I never had the opportunity to do as a kid." Michael looked back at Savannah in the rearview mirror. "Is that your phone, hon?" he asked.

"Yes," she said, looking at the screen. "It's my sister. Hi Bri, what's up? You guys coming down?"

"Hi, Sis. Yeah, we're heading that way now."

"Tonight?" Savannah asked.

"Uh-huh. We're stopping in Santa Barbara or Ventura overnight and we'll show up in the morning around nine or ten."

"Great! We're looking forward to seeing you. We're on our way home from Disneyland."

"Cool. So you're having a good time?"

"Wonderful. Weather's super. House is perfect. Can't wait to share it all with you. Oh, Bri, what day are you heading back?"

"Want to get rid of us already?" Brianna asked, laughing.

"No. We're just trying to figure a way to get Adam home. His folks have some family plans later in the week."

"We have to leave Wednesday. Will that work?" Brianna asked. "We'd be happy to give Adam a lift."

Savannah smiled. "Great. Sure appreciate it—I know Marci and Eric do, too."

"Can't wait. I love spending time with that kid."

"See you tomorrow. Hey, did you pack a nice dress? We're going to a fancy show for Peter tomorrow night."

Savannah heard silence on the other end of the phone. Finally Brianna said, "Uh, no, did you tell me that? If so, I forgot."

"I guess I forgot, too. No problem, we'll go shopping."

"Okay. See you tomorrow, then."

***

The next morning, Peter strolled into the main part of the house around nine and found Michael and Adam on the deck munching on cookies and drinking milk.

"Milk and cookies for breakfast?" he asked, when he joined them.

"Yeah, want some?" Michael offered.

"Sure do. Thanks." He addressed Adam: "So you liked Disneyland, did you?"

The boy's face lit up. "Yes, it was awesome!"

"Good morning," Savannah said, yawning as she joined the others on the deck with Lily in her arms. "Why didn't you wake me? I missed the sunrise."

"Sorry, hon; figured you'd like to sleep in. You have a big day planned."

"Sure do—what time tonight and where?" Savannah asked Peter.

"I'll have the driver pick us up at seven."

"Driver?" Savannah asked.

"Yes, we're arriving by limo." Peter looked at Michael and then Savannah. "Blake will be with us tonight."

Savannah smiled. "Oh, good. I'd like to meet her."

"My phone," Peter said, edging it out of his pocket. He walked away to answer it. When he returned, he said, "Well, that's just darn weird."

"What?" Savannah and Michael asked.

"Whales!" Adam hollered. "Look, a bunch of whales!"

Michael laughed. "No, those are dolphins, Son. They come to visit us most mornings. Cool, aren't they? Sometimes they ride the waves like surfers."

"Can I go down to the beach and look at them closer?" the boy asked, excitedly.

"Sure. Take the binoculars, if you want."

"Okay," he said, grabbing them off a nearby table. "Can Lexie go with me?"

"Uh…yes," Michael said, reaching for her leash and handing it to the boy.

"Come on, Lexie," Adam said, rushing with her down the steps and onto the beach.

"What a whirlwind of energy, that son of mine," Michael said, chuckling. He then focused on Peter. "So everything okay?"

He frowned. "No. That was Dawna. She wanted to give me a heads-up before I came in—said sales were slow yesterday. That doesn't make sense," he said. "There was a big convention going on and one of their tour stops was my gallery. I spent a lot on an advertisement in their program. Should have sold $10,000 at the very least. Dawna said sales amounted to less than $2,000. Man, that's a blow." He ran his hand through his black hair. "What is going on? I've had as much as $30,000 in paintings go out the door when we've done this sort of promotion." He sighed deeply. "Well, it leaves me more paintings to display at the mansion this evening, I guess. Hopefully, some of them will sell there.”

“Gosh, that’s bizarre,” Michael said. “Maybe sales were down yesterday because you weren’t there—people would rather buy from the artist.”

“I don’t think that’s it. Dawna was on the floor yesterday and she’s an amazing salesperson. I’ve watched her turn a casual browser into the owner of one of my paintings. She’s got what it takes. Kara, too. She’s young, but she does a good job in sales.”

“Maybe you pegged the group wrong,” Savannah suggested.

“What?” Peter asked.

“Could be that the folks attending that convention don’t have money or the type of homes for art like yours.”

“Naw, that’s not it. These were corporate leaders. Oh yes, they have the means.” He shook his head. “Well, I’d better get down to the gallery and survey the damages. See you this evening at seven if not before.”

“Can I take Rags for a walk, now?” Adam asked, bounding up the steps to the deck with Lexie.

Michael and Savannah looked at each other. “Yeah, I guess,” she said. “I don’t know if he’s ever walked on sand.”

“Well, yes, he has,” Michael said, grinning. “He walks in sand every day.”

Savannah looked confused and then she exclaimed, “Oh, I guess he does! You mean in his litter box.” She handed the baby to Michael. “I’ll go get his harness and leash.”

“What do you want for breakfast?” Gladys asked, joining the others on the deck.

“Morning, Mom. Sleep well?”

"Really good," she said. "I'm not used to traipsing all over a theme park like that. I was so tired, I thought I'd sleep for a week."

"Sorry, Gladys; was it too much?" Michael asked. "Didn't mean to wear you out."

Her eyes widened. "No, I had a great time. It was a good tired. No, Michael, I wouldn't have missed it for the world."

Well, good, then," he said. "Breakfast? Adam and I've been munching on those cookies Peter's housekeeper made and washing them down with milk. Anyway, we didn't invite you here to wait on us."

"Don't mind a bit. I miss cooking for my family." She giggled a little, as if she had a secret, saying, "I'm having fun in that big kitchen with all those gadgets."

Savannah returned from the house with Rags in his harness, handed the leash to Adam, and told him, "Stay where we can see you."

"Okay." He looked up at her. "That means where I can see you, right?"

"Right, buddy," Michael said.

"How about a veggie omelet, or do you want blueberry pancakes?" Gladys asked.

"The omelet sound good to me," Michael said, glancing at Savannah.

"Perfect," she said. "I'll help, Mom. Michael, do you want to feed Lily her cereal and applesauce?"

"Sure do," he said, smiling at the baby. He set her in her chair and began feeding her the mixture Savannah handed him.

After Gladys and Savannah carried the omelets and toast out to the umbrella table, Savannah walked to the edge of the deck to look for Adam. She saw a group of people gathered a short distance away, and shaded her eyes and squinted in that direction. "Michael," she said, "Adam seems to have a crowd around him. Why don't you go check and see what's going on—have him come eat his breakfast, would you?"

When Michael approached the group of about eight people, he spotted Adam and Rags among them. Everyone seemed to be staring down at the cat. Some were snapping pictures with their cell phones.

"Hi, Dad," Adam said. "Rags is famous!"

Before Michael could respond, he heard, "Hi there, Michael."

"Oh, Sidney…Glenn, hi." He looked around at the others. "What's going on?"

"Just introducing Rags to my family," Sidney said. "They've never met a celebrity cat before."

"Yeah Dad, Sidney hid a dollar and Rags dug it up." He leaned toward Michael as if sharing a secret. "I think he's showing off."

"Yes, he does like an audience," Michael said, chuckling. "Hey, buddy, it's time for breakfast. Wanna bring the world-famous cat back to the house?"

"Okay," he said. "Come on Rags."

"Hey, cool cat," a teen among the group said. "He's not even afraid of the water."

"Maybe you could teach him to surf and get rich showing his video on YouTube," one young woman suggested. "Rags could go viral."

"Thanks for sharing," another one called out.

"You're welcome. Glad you enjoyed him," Michael said, turning and walking with Adam and the cat back to the house.

"Hey, Bri and Bud are here!" Adam said as they approached the deck. "Hi!" he called out. "I'm taking Rags for a walk."

"Hi there, cutie," Brianna said, walking to the edge of the deck to greet Adam and Michael. "Great place, Michael," she said, hugging him briefly.

"Welcome to our dream vacation, Bri," he said.

"Say hello to Rags," Adam prompted.

"Hi, old boy. Been in any trouble lately?" she asked, ruffling the fur on the cat's head.

"He's escaped twice, so far," Savannah said, walking up behind her sister.

"Hi Bud," Michael greeted. "Everything okay at the clinic?"

"No problems there," he said. "It's been fairly quiet, actually."

"That's good. Glad you could get away. How do your folks manage out at the ranch when you're gone?"

"They do okay. They hired a couple of hands when I went full-time at the clinic, so my chores at the place have diminished some."

"Did you eat? Want a veggie omelet?" Gladys asked the couple.

"Sounds wonderful," Brianna said.

Bud nodded.

Once everyone had eaten, Savannah announced, "Bri and I are going shopping. Anyone want to come with us?"

Michael looked at Adam and winked. "Want to go shopping, buddy?"

The boy looked down and glanced quickly up at Michael and then Savannah. "Um…"

"Well, I don't," Michael said. "I want to stay here and maybe do some boogie-boarding and body-surfing and play Frisbee."

Adam's face brightened into a wide smile. "Me, too. That's what I want to do."

"Sound good?" Michael asked Bud.

"Hey, I'm in," he said.

"What about you, Mom?" Savannah asked.

She thought for a moment and said, "I think I'll just hang out here with Lilliana. You don't want to drag her all over town after our big day at Disneyland, do you?"

"Probably not," Savannah agreed. "If that's what you want to do, that would be great."

"Truly it is. I'm enjoying being a grandmamma, and I have a couple of books on my Kindle for when she takes her nap," Gladys said.

Savannah looked at Brianna. "I guess it's just you and me."

"Cool. Sistah time. When do you want to go?"

"Well, I promised Adam we'd build a sand castle this morning." She punched her sister in the arm playfully and said, "How about let's get sandy, then we can clean up around noon and head out for the shops."

Brianna smiled. "Great, I'll go put on my suit."

"Oh yes, let me show you to your room," Savannah offered, looping her arm in her sister's.

Brianna motioned to Bud. "Come on, babe. Bring our bags, would you?"

"An ocean view!" Brianna exclaimed.

"Cool," Bud said.

Brianna looked around. "And our own little deck and attached bath. I love it! I also like that little fish print on the bedspread. Makes me feel like a kid again."

80

A short time later, Brianna emerged from the house. "Bri, you look good in that suit," Savannah said. "I love it on you. And by the way, I like your hair straightened like that."

"Yeah, but I'll be curly by noon in this ocean air," she complained.

"You were meant to have curls," Gladys snapped, "yet, you've always fought them." She stepped back and studied her younger daughter for a moment. "Honey, you look like I did when I was young. You still have a nice figure, which isn't easy when you're built like we are."

Brianna smirked in Savannah's direction. "Yeah, then there's skinny Minnie, stilt-woman."

"Come on, it's not always easy being taller than everyone else," Savannah said. "It's hard to find slacks long enough in my size. Tall women can look kind of awkward and disjointed."

Brianna laughed. "Yeah, but you can reach things we can't reach, see over heads in a crowd, break through the finish line first with those long legs…"

Savannah sighed. "I guess we all have our assets and our shortcomings. I mean, you have the beautiful Brannon skin. I have freckles and stick-straight hair."

"Oh boo-hoo. You wouldn't know what to do with curly hair if you had it. It's a hassle, I'm telling you."

"Not if you just let it go natural," Gladys said. She gave her daughter a disgusted look. "But you interfere with nature by straightening it."

"Are you guys mad at each other?" Adam asked, wide-eyed.

The three women turned toward him and noticed a look of concern on his face.

"No," Savannah said, laughing. "We're just having a…"

"Family discussion," Brianna said, smiling.

Adam continued to look confused. When he glanced at his father, Michael winked at him, saying, "It's a girl thing."

"Okay." He looked up at Savannah expectantly. "Are you ready to build a sand castle?"

"Sure am," Savannah said. She glanced at her mother. "Are you going to help us?"

Gladys thought about the invitation for a moment. "I might bring the baby down and watch you."

"Here, I'll carry a chair for you," Savannah offered.

An hour and a half later, the three women walked back up the deck steps with Adam.

"You should have seen it, Dad," Adam said. "It was awesome and then a wave came and wrecked the whole thing."

"Well, I have a surprise for you, buddy," Michael said.

"What?"

"I took pictures of it. Wanna see?"

"Yeah!" Adam shouted. "Hey, Dad's got pictures! Come look, Savannah, Aunt Bri, Grandma."

"It's a video, actually," Michael said. He pushed a few buttons on his phone. "Are you ready for this?"

"Yeah!" Adam said

Brianna cringed. "Oh, I'm afraid to look."

"Drum roll. Here it is," Michael said, handing his phone to Adam.

The three women stood behind the boy and stared into the screen.

"Hey, there it is," Adam said. "Awesome! And we didn't even know you were taking pictures of us, Dad."

"Yeah, thanks a lot," Brianna said, sarcastically, pulling her cover-up tighter around herself.

"There *you* are, Aunt Bri, trying to get that seaweed decoration out of the water," Adam said, laughing.

"Yeah, from the back. Lordy, Michael, I owe you one," she said, scowling.

Savanna chuckled. "Oh, you look cute."

Suddenly, Brianna began to laugh. "So do you, Sis. Real cute." She roared with laughter. "I see what you mean about being awkward."

"Huh?" Savannah asked, looking at the phone screen. "Michael!" she scolded. "What were you thinking? Erase that this minute," she demanded.

"Wait," Bud said, "I want to see it."

Savannah put her hand over the phone screen. "Just you never mind."

Adam giggled. "It was pretty funny, Savannah, when that wave knocked you down."

"Yes," Brianna said, "it certainly was."

"How'd I miss that?" Gladys asked.

"Just never mind," Savannah said. "Now, Bri, if you want to go shopping with me, you'd better be in the living room in fifteen minutes."

"Fifteen minutes?" Brianna complained.

"Sharp," Savannah said.

"Here Vannie, tell your daughter goodnight," Gladys said, holding the baby toward her. "I'll feed her and put her down for her nap."

Savannah took the baby from her mother and hugged and kissed her. She blew raspberries on her neck and made her giggle. She then kissed the baby's chubby hands and said, before handing Lily back to her grandmother, "'Bye my angel. Mommy loves you."

Brianna tweaked the baby's toes, saying, "You are such a doll baby." She kissed Lily on the cheek and then let out a yelp. "Let go!" she said. "Let go!"

Savannah and Gladys began to laugh as they attempted to pry the baby's chubby hands from around strands of Brianna's hair. "No, no, Lily," Savannah said between fits of laughter.

Once Brianna was free of the baby's grip, Gladys said, still laughing, "I guess she was trying to help you straighten it back out."

"Or she wants your curls," Savannah said. She looked more closely at her sister's hair. "It *is* getting curly, isn't it? That's from the damp air?"

"Yup, humidity is my enemy," Brianna said, pulling on some of the strands that were starting to kink.

"Maybe for your hair," Savannah said, "but it does wonders for your skin."

***

By twelve thirty, Savannah and Brianna had walked to the nearest shopping district in the beach community.

"This is so quaint," Brianna said. "I love it." She looked at her sister. "So what am I looking for? What are you wearing?"

"My little black dress with pearls," Savannah said.

Brianna cast her eyes downward. "Oh."

"What's wrong?" Savannah asked.

"I'll never look as good as you, no matter what I try on," she whined. She exaggerated a pout. "This is going to be an absolute disaster."

Savannah sighed. "Now that's no way to approach a shopping trip." She looped her arm through Brianna's and led her into the closest store. "Come on, let's check out this place."

After they'd looked at practically everything on the racks in Brianna's size, they walked out. They entered the next store and had the same experience.

"You're too fussy," Savannah said.

"I don't see anything that's me," Brianna complained.

Savannah sighed impatiently. "Well, I think there's only one more dress shop. If you don't find something you like here, we can get in the car and head for the mall. What designers do you usually wear?"

"I don't know—whatever fits and I'm comfortable in. Oh look," she said, pointing to a dress on display in another store window. "I like that one."

Savannah smirked. "That would not look good on you."

"What makes you think so?"

"Well, I'm pretty sure, but go ahead and try it." After several minutes, Brianna walked out of the dressing room carrying the dress.

"What do you think?" Savannah asked.

"I love it!"

"Really?" Savannah said, disbelieving.

"It looks smashing."

"Why didn't you model it for me?" Savannah wanted to know.

Brianna smirked. "Didn't want your negative input." She put her hand on Savannah's arm. "I'll show it to you this evening. You'll get the reveal then."

"Okay," Savannah said, apprehensively. She then asked, "Want lunch? My treat."

Brianna shook her head. "Oh no, I'll treat since you're letting us enjoy your vacation home."

"Now that's not necessary—I'm so glad you could make it."

"I feel that we owe you for including us."

"But…oh my gosh!" Savannah said, grabbing Brianna's arm.

Brianna gasped. "What?" she asked, fear in her eyes.

"Come on. I want to check something out. Let's cross here," she said, pulling her sister along as she launched out into the street.

"Watch out!" Brianna said, glancing at the oncoming cars. "You'll get us killed. At least wait until after this glorious weekend," she whined.

Once on the other side of the street, Savannah led her sister up a ways and then stopped in front of a homeless man who was sitting on a small plot of grass between two buildings.

"What are you doing?" Brianna whispered rather loudly. "Do you know him?"

"Excuse me," Savannah said to the man. "That painting…may I ask where you got it?"

The man squinted up at Savannah through long stringy strands of blond hair. "It's mine. I found it," he said. He smiled, revealing that he was missing several teeth, and asked, "Wanna buy it? You can have it for twenty bucks."

"I might buy it. But first, I want to know where you *found* it."

"Why? What does it matter?"

"Because I think you stole it. Did you steal it? I'm not buying any stolen goods," Savannah said.

Brianna's eyes became saucers. "Vannie, what are you doing. Come on," she said, trying to pull her away.

Savannah shook her sister's hand loose, telling her, "Just a minute—it's okay." She then addressed the man again. "So, did you steal it?"

"No, I told ya, I found it."

"Where?" she insisted. When he hesitated, she said, "Hey, I saw a cop just around the corner. I can have him here in a hot minute."

He looked around, his eyes wide. "Okay, I dug it out of a Dumpster, and that's no lie. Someone else must have stole it. But it wasn't me."

"What Dumpster?" Savannah pushed.

"About two blocks up behind those art places…"

"Galleries?"

"Yeah, galleries." He leaned toward Savannah and looked in both directions before speaking. "I saw someone toss it in there and I dug it out, that's all. I thought it was purty and figured I could sell it."

"What did the person look like?"

"Hell, lady, I don't know. It was dark, ya know. I didn't get a good look at him. He didn't see me. I pretended to be asleep."

Savannah hesitated and then asked, "Did you see where he went?"

"No, didn't notice that. I was pretending to be asleep, remember? He just disappeared—I guess walked on down the street or somethin'."

"Okay, so you say you want twenty for it?"

The man perked up. "Yeah. You wanna buy it?"

"Yes," she said, digging into her purse. She handed him the money, then took the painting. "Thanks," she mumbled as the two women walked away.

"Why did you do that?" Brianna asked, trying to keep up with her sister as she walked swiftly down the street.

Savannah, her jaw set in staunch determination, said, "Because this is one of Peter's paintings."

# Chapter 3

"Where are we going?" Brianna insisted. "Why are you walking so fast? Remember, my legs aren't as long as yours."

"Oh, sorry. I just want to get this back to Peter. We can slow down. We're almost there, anyway."

When the two women entered the gallery, they saw Peter dusting a panel of paintings.

He looked up. "Oh hi, Savannah." He gazed at Brianna.

"Hi, Peter," she responded. "This is my sister Brianna."

"Nice to meet you." Peter looked from one to the other of the women. "Sisters, huh?"

Brianna quipped, "Yeah, same mother, same father, but the genes organized in totally different ways."

"Well," he said, smiling, "you certainly are two beautiful women, but with strikingly different assets."

"Spoken like an artist," Brianna said, chuckling. She bowed her head. "Thank you." She then narrowed her eyes. "…I think."

"Whatcha got there?" he asked. When Savannah turned the painting to face him, he frowned, appearing confused. "Well, where did you get that?" he asked, taking it from her.

Just then, Dawna walked in from the back room. She greeted Savannah briefly, glanced at Brianna, and then said to Peter, "I need to speak to you." When she saw what he held in his hands, she asked, "Where did that come from…I mean…where did you find it?"

He nodded toward the two women. "Savannah was just about to tell me."

"Well, I bought it from a man in an alley for twenty bucks," she said.

Peter looked stunned. "What? How did he…?" he muttered, shaking his head slowly back and forth.

"Oh, those homeless are always hanging around here," Dawna said. "Probably snuck in the back door and grabbed it."

Peter spoke sternly to Dawna. "We can't have the art sitting around back there with the door open. You know that."

"Yeah, well, those teeny-boppers you have working here probably forgot," Dawna snapped.

"Maybe that isn't how he got it at all," Peter said. He examined the painting more closely. "He may have ripped it off from someone who bought it here. That's always a possibility."

"Well, he says he found it in a Dumpster out back," Savannah said. "Says he saw some guy toss it in there."

"Some guy?" Dawna repeated. "Oh, you can't believe what those homeless say. They all lie."

Just then a couple walked into the gallery. "Come with me," Peter said, motioning to Savannah and Brianna. The trio walked into the back room. "Thanks for bringing this in," he said. He chuckled. "You got yourself quite a deal there. This painting should bring $800 or more." He then reached into his pocket, pulled out a twenty, and handed it to Savannah.

She put her hand up in front of her. "Consider it a down payment on the painting I'm going to buy." When he looked puzzled, she said, "Well, I haven't decided which one, but I have my eye on that ocean scene—looks sort of like a spot I love in Big Sur."

"Oh, I know the one," he said. "I'll set it aside for you, if you're serious."

"It's my favorite so far. But I haven't seen them all."

"You sure do beautiful work," Brianna said. "I love all the detail and the way you kind of swirl it all together to create a story."

"Thank you," he said. "Are you a writer?"

She smiled. "No. I'm a doctor."

He raised his eyebrows. "Oh, a doctor? Well, you should write art reviews. That one was unique."

"So is your art," Brianna said, smiling demurely.

***

"I hear you had some excitement today," Michael said to Brianna as they gathered in the living room before leaving that evening.

"Yes, your wife is something else. She thinks she's some sort of investigator or private eye," she said. "She practically wrestled some guy to the ground to get that stupid painting back."

"Wrestled him to the ground?" Bud repeated, his eyes wide.

"That is a gross exaggeration," Savannah insisted. "I merely retrieved one of Peter's stolen paintings for him. And it cost me twenty bucks, too."

*Knock-knock.*

"That must be our driver," Michael said. "Good-bye, Gladys. See you later, Son. Don't beat Grandma too bad at checkers."

Adam smiled at Gladys. "I won't."

Gladys waved to the group as they left. "You all have a nice time."

"Love that dress on you, Sis," Savannah said, stepping out through the door. "You were right. You did good."

"Yes, you look great," Bud said as they approached the limo. He glanced at Savannah and Michael. "I guess we should go out more often. I don't get to see her all dressed up."

"And what about you?" Michael said. "When's the last time you wore a dress shirt?"

"Probably the last wedding I attended. I'm glad Peter has a friend my size. I look good in this jacket, don't you think?" he asked, grinning.

Brianna smiled at him. "Sure do, babe."

"Good evening, everyone," Peter said from inside the limousine. "Pile in, there's plenty of room." Once everyone was seated, he introduced Blake, a willowy woman with long black hair framing an expertly made-up face.

"You're a PI?" Michael asked, disbelieving.

"Michael," Savannah scolded, "pretty women can be capable, too."

"Uh, oh, I didn't mean to sound like...I mean..."

"Better stop while you're…um, behind, Michael," Peter said, laughing.

The group arrived at the location twenty minutes later. After exiting the car, they were ushered directly into the mansion. "Gosh this is some place," Brianna said, looking around wide-eyed.

"Boy, is it ever," Savannah agreed. "Wouldn't want to clean it."

Brianna smirked at her sister. "Spoken like a homemaker."

"Follow the arrows to the gallery," the greeter invited.

"How cool," Bud said, "…a red carpet with arrows."

"Oh, Peter," Savannah said, once they'd entered the temporary gallery, "look at all the paintings. They're all yours?"

"Well, yes," he said.

"It's just that there are so many."

He smiled and shrugged. "I'm prolific; what can I tell you?"

After they toured the expansive gallery, they entered another part of the home, where they found dozens of people dressed in exquisite designer clothes, wearing expensive jewelry, and sipping cocktails while nibbling on fancy hors d'oeuvres.

"Where's your right and left hand?" Savannah asked when she had the opportunity.

"Long story," Peter said.  Just then they heard a gentle chiming sound. "Know what that means?" Peter asked those standing around him.

The individuals in the group shook their heads.

"It means we sold a painting. One chime is $100 for charity. Two is $500."

"Wow, nice," Savannah said.

Peter nodded. "Music to my ears."

Just then, a well-dressed older man, who looked quite comfortable in his jeans and expensive sport coat, walked up. "Hello, Peter, my boy," he said. He nodded to the people standing around the artist.

Peter grabbed the man's outstretched hand. "Hey, Felix. Good to see you! Meet some of my friends." He introduced Blake, the Iveys, and Bri and Bud.

After greeting each of them, Felix turned to Peter. "Is everything okay?"

"Yeah, why?" Peter asked.

Felix rubbed the back of his neck. "Just wondering why you're showing other artists' work in your gallery."

"What?" Peter said, obviously too loud. He squinted and asked, "What do you mean, Felix?"

"Well, Friday, Meela wandered into your gallery with her cousin who's visiting from Spain and none of your work was hanging. It was someone else's work—some of it was close to your style, but Meela knows your work."

"Of course she does." Peter frowned. He shook his head. "Someone else's work?" he asked. "That's…well, I don't know what to say, except she must be mistaken."

Felix made eye contact. "I don't think so, Peter."

"I just don't get it. I was gone all day Friday. Dawna was in charge…"

Felix nodded. "Yes, Meela said she was there. Dawna was taking care of a customer, so she didn't speak with her. In fact, the place was pretty busy, so Meela just left. She said she saw a couple of tour buses in the neighborhood."

Peter scratched his head. "We were expecting a crowd that day."

*Chime-Chime*

"Cool," Felix said to Peter. "More for the charity and more for your pockets."

Peter nodded without much expression. He noticed that Blake was engaged in conversation with a couple at the bar and he took the opportunity to excuse himself.

As he left, Brianna turned to her sister. "Vannie, I want one of those paintings for my office. I actually saw one I like. Wanna go with me to see if we can find it? Let's make some music, shall we?"

"Sure. Sounds fun," Savannah agreed.

The two women were halfway to the gallery when they heard someone shouting. Savannah stopped. "Who's that?" she asked, not expecting an answer.

"Hell if I know," Brianna said. "Sure sounds mad." She tugged on Savannah's arm. "Let's get out of here."

Savannah pulled away and eased quietly toward a partially open door. "It's Peter," she whispered, when she saw him in the dim light, pacing and shouting into his cell phone. She frowned and quietly closed the door, urging Brianna along toward the gallery.

"It's this one," Brianna said, pointing. "Wouldn't that be a peaceful scene to hang in the waiting room?"

"Oh yes," Savannah agreed. "The colors are marvelously soothing. I love it. Good choice, Sis."

Brianna looked around. "I wonder who I pay."

Just then a plump woman in a purple knit dress and a gaudy necklace approached them. "Are you buying it?" she asked.

Brianna nodded.

The woman chuckled. "Just follow me." She glanced back at Savannah. "Are you buying, too?"

"The one I want is in the gallery at the beach," she said. "I think he set it aside for me."

"Well, dear, when you purchase it, you can request that a percentage of the proceeds go to the charity. Everything sold through Sunday night supports the charity."

"Oh, good. I'll try to purchase it by then," she promised.

Once Brianna had paid for the painting, they watched as an elderly gentleman stood up from his chair and struck the chimes, which could be heard throughout the home.

"Exciting," Brianna said. She turned to the woman. "So how will you keep someone else from buying it? Do I take it now or what?"

The woman laughed. "No, we'll put a sold sticker on it. See, like this one," she said, pointing.

"Oh. Okay. I guess I'll come get it before I leave, right?"

"You can do that or we'll deliver it to you, if it won't fit in your car."

Brianna looked at the painting again. "I think it'll fit—we're in a limo with the artist," she bragged.

When the sisters rejoined Michael and Bud, the men were chatting with Peter, Blake, and another couple. Savannah shot a quick look at Peter, who seemed to have recovered nicely from his outburst on the cell phone.

"I bought a painting," Brianna announced.

"You did?" Bud asked. "For your office?"

Brianna nodded.

"Which one?" Peter asked.

"*Golden Fields*," she said. "I love the colors filtering through the trees into that meadow. I'm going to hang it in my waiting room."

"Oh yes," he said. He reached for Brianna's hand and bowed slightly, saying, "Thank you. I hope your patients enjoy it as much as I enjoyed painting it."

"There was a magician in here a minute ago," Bud said.

Blake added, "And there's a wandering violinist. She's superb."

"I hear there are acrobats on one of the patios," Peter said.

"Where?" Brianna asked. "I love acrobats."

Peter raised a hand and motioned to one of several young women who were dressed in old-fashioned bellman outfits. When she walked up to the group, Peter asked, "Where are the acrobats performing?"

She pointed, using her whole arm like a traffic cop. "Out that door, sir, and to the left." She pointed in another direction. "There's a juggling act on the south lawn. And in the east gardens, you can enjoy a harpist."

Brianna clasped her hands together. "Gosh, which one do I want to see first?"

Bud pointed toward the open French doors. "Well, let's just wander out that way and see what we see, shall we?"

"Okay," she said. She turned toward the others. "Coming?"

Savannah glanced at Michael and then Peter and Blake. "I'd like to," she said, taking Michael's arm. They followed Bud and Brianna; the others trailed along behind. They enjoyed several of the acts before strolling out to hear the harpist. They'd been seated in chairs around a small rose garden for fifteen minutes or so when Savannah's eyes began to wander. Suddenly, in the distance, she thought she saw someone familiar. *Oh, it's Kara,* she noticed, *and Charlynn's with her. They seem to be looking for someone. Probably Peter. I'll try to get their attention and let them know where we are.* Suddenly she scowled. *What are they doing?* she wondered. She watched as the two women glanced around and then moved quickly behind a row of shrubs. Savannah soon realized she was probably the only one who could see them and it was obvious that the women had not noticed her watching them.

*They're taking something out of a tote bag. It looks like a painting. What's that Kara has in her hand—a spray can?* Savannah squinted into the dimness of the night. *Well, it looks like they're spraying something all over that painting. I wonder why?*

Suddenly, she saw Charlynn shove the framed item under the shrub. Kara tossed the spray can and the two of them walked out into a more well-lighted area. *They're giggling like a couple of teenagers,* Savannah noticed. *I wonder what that was all about.* She glanced at Peter. *Should I tell him what I saw? Should I confront the gals? Or should I do as Michael would probably suggest and just stay out of it?*

As if confirming her thoughts, Michael reached over and took Savannah's hand, holding it while the music continued.

***

"Will you sign it?" Brianna asked Peter on the ride home in the limo later that night.

"Well, Bri, it's signed, see?" Savannah pointed at the lower right-hand corner of the painting.

"Yes, but I want him to sign it on the back, too."

"Yeah, I can do that," Peter said, pulling a felt pen out of his jacket pocket.

"Came prepared, huh?" Michael teased.

"Yeah, didn't you see him autographing napkins and programs and things for people tonight?" Brianna asked.

Blake chuckled. "…and a woman's tattoo."

"No, I was *enhancing* her tattoo," Peter explained. "She told me she thought my art was better than her former boyfriend's. He's a tattoo artist."

"Oh?" she said.

"Yeah, so she pulls up her dress and shows me this tattoo on her thigh. You know I'd had a little bit to drink…"

"A little bit?" Blake questioned, smiling.

"Uh-huh, so I offered to enhance her tattoo with my artistic flair," he said, motioning dramatically with his pen in the air.

This has been a wonderful evening," Savannah said. "Thanks for including us."

"Yes," Brianna said. "I had such a good time."

"Me, too," Bud agreed. "I don't think I've ever been to such a fancy shindig that was so…entertaining."

"Nope, in our neck of the woods, a barn dance is a big deal," Michael said, laughing. "Peter, you'll have to come visit us sometime. We'll show you how to party down hillbilly style."

Peter grinned. "You guys jest, but hey, I'd like to share in your lifestyle—that would be a vacation for me."

"Oh my gosh, Michael," Savannah gasped, as they pulled up in front of the beach house.

"What?"

"Is that Rags? Dang, he's outside again."

"That's him," Michael said, shaking his head. "That knucklehead. What does he think he's doing? How does he keep escaping?"

Peter peered out the window and started to laugh. He said to Blake, "They have the coolest cat. He steals things."

"Really?" she said. "I've heard of kleptomaniac cats, but I've never met one."

"Well, come on," Savannah invited. "Shall we have a nightcap before you head home, Blake?"

Michael nudged Savannah with his elbow. "Oh, or maybe you're not going home…" Completely embarrassed now, she took a deep breath and said, "Well, let's go get our cat. Do come in and meet him."

"Looks like he has something in his mouth," Blake said, squinting a little.

Savannah looked out at him again. "Yes, he does. Darn it."

Brianna shook her head slowly. "That crazy cat."

"He solved a murder that happened at our clinic once," Bud reported.

"Oh, he's the one I read about that helps the police department," Blake said, excitedly. She laughed. "Hey, I could sure use a cat like him in my line of work."

"Michael, would you get him?" Savannah asked, when the limo had stopped. "I can't run in these heels."

Michael called to the cat, who glanced toward the limo, hopped up on the porch steps, and sat down, staring at the front door. When Michael opened it, Rags picked something up off the porch and marched into the house with it in his mouth.

"What is it?" Brianna asked, as they all rushed through the door.

"I think it's jewelry," Blake said. "Looks like a pearl necklace."

"Close," Michael said, grabbing the cat and taking it from him. "It's shells. A shell necklace."

"That's odd," Peter said, furrowing his brow.

"What?" Savannah asked.

"Well, Dawna bought a necklace like that just today from a couple of young girls who came into the gallery. Let me see it."

Before handing it over, Michael looked more closely at it. "There's something all over it—paint or something."

Peter started to take the necklace from Michael, when Blake said, "No. Give me your pen, Peter." She took it and reached out, looping the necklace over the pen. "Blood," she said, upon closer examination.

"What?" Michael and Savannah said in unison.

Blake made eye contact with some of the others. "That's blood splattered on the shells."

"Did he kill for that piece of jewelry?" Peter asked, laughing.

"That's not funny, Peter," Michael said, chuckling a little. "He has a record, but he's never been booked for anything that serious."

"Can you identify this, Peter?" Blake asked.

"Uh, well, I don't know. I mean those shell necklaces are a dime a dozen in this area." He stared at it intently, then said, "Wait. There was one thing Dawna showed me." He stooped to get a better look at the necklace that Blake held up. "There it is," he said, his voice raised slightly in anxiety. "See that little face on that one shell?"

"Face?" Blake said, peering at the necklace more closely.

"Yes, if you look at it from just the right angle, you'll see an Asian-looking face inside one of the big shells. The girls had a story behind that phenomenon—said it occurs like one in a thousand shells."

"Or they painted it on there as a selling point," Brianna said.

Peter took a step back. He appeared shaken. "I think that's Dawna's necklace. But how did the cat get it?"

"Maybe she came here looking for you and dropped it outside," Brianna suggested. She leaned in and examined it carefully. "Doesn't appear to be broken." She turned toward Savannah and Michael. "Can he unfasten jewelry clasps?"

They both shook their head. "Not that I know of," she said.

"She wouldn't come here tonight," Peter said. "She knew I wasn't here. She arranged the charity gig, for Pete's sake."

"Doesn't she live near here?" Blake asked. "You showed me her place; seems like it was in this area."

"Yeah," Peter said, "she has an apartment north of here, about a block over."

"That *is* close," Blake said. "Think we ought to check on her?"

"Why?"

"Because that's blood on the necklace and if this is hers, she could be in trouble. Maybe she had an accident or something," she reasoned.

Peter thought about it for a moment. "Let's go," he said.

"Do you have an envelope I could put this thing in?" Blake asked.

"I think so," Peter said. "I'll get one."

"Can we come?" Brianna asked, rather eagerly.

Blake looked around at the others and shrugged. "Sure, okay with me."

Savannah started to rush toward the stairs, saying, "Let me get my comfy shoes."

"Me, too," Brianna said, heading down the hallway.

Savannah stopped before taking the stairs and looked at Blake's feet. "What size do you wear?"

Blake dropped the necklace into the envelope Peter had handed her and then quickly flashed one hand at

Savannah twice, indicating size ten.

"Perfect," Savannah said. When she returned, she had two pairs of flip-flops and offered Blake her choice.

She reached for a pair and then quipped. "These go better with my dress."

Michael looked at Bud. "How about we stay here and chug down some beers on the deck?"

"Hey, my kind of invitation," he said.

"Take good care of the girls," Michael called to Peter.

"Sure will," he said, glancing in the direction of the three women.

Bud started to step out onto the deck, stopped, and asked, "Got your phone, Brianna?" Suddenly, both Savannah and Brianna scurried away in search of their cell phones, rejoining Peter and Blake within seconds.

"This is a bloody long walk for a cat," Blake said. She flashed Savannah a smile. "Thanks, by the way, for the flip-flops. I don't walk much in heels."

"Really?" Savannah questioned. "You seem so at home in them."

"Naw," she said. "I can look like a Barbie, but I'm really more the Dora type."

Brianna appeared puzzled. "Dora?"

Savannah responded. "She's a more down-to-earth, realistic, smart role-model for young girls who don't buy into the princess thing."

Brianna shrugged.

"There's her place," Peter said, walking faster than the others.

"The one with the light on?" Brianna asked.

"Look, there's no screen on that open window," Savannah observed. "Gosh, I hope she's okay."

The quartet walked up the stairs to Dawna's apartment door. Peter knocked. He knocked harder and called out. When he didn't hear a response, he tried the door. Locked. That's when he reached into his pocket and pulled out a key ring. "In case of emergency," he said, defending the fact that he had Dawna's house key. "This could be an emergency."

Once inside, Savannah and Brianna hung back and Peter and Blake disappeared into another room. Within seconds, the sisters heard, "Oh my God!! No!!"

Blake returned to the living room. She was on her phone. "9.1.1, we need an ambulance. Stat! Yeah, it looks like a woman was attacked in her home. She's losing blood fast. Address?" she looked at Savannah, who rushed outside.

"1842…" she said, reporting the numbers on the building. She hesitated, straining to see the street sign.

Brianna walked down a few steps and leaned over the railing. She squinted to see the sign in the dim street lights. "Dolphin Street."

"Apartment six," Savannah added, looking at the open front door.

Blake relayed the information to the dispatcher and then rejoined Peter in the next room.

"Michael," Savannah said quietly into her phone from the porch, "Dawna is hurt in there. That might have been her necklace that Rags had. Paramedics are on their way. Oh, I hear them."

"So do I, hon," he said into the phone. He hesitated and added, "Bud and I are going to walk out and meet you two. Where are you?"

"Take our street south to Seahorse and turn left. It's the green apartments just up from the corner of Seahorse and Dolphin. We'll head that way." Before leaving, Savannah stepped inside the front door and called out to Peter and Blake, "They're on their way. We're going back home. Anything you need us to do?"

"No. Thanks anyway," Peter said. When he stepped into the doorway, Savannah saw blood on his clothes. He was obviously distraught. "You know, the police might have questions. If so, I'll send them down to the house, okay?"

"Sure," Savannah said.

Peter started to step back into the other room when he stopped and said, "Tell your cat thanks. He may have saved her life."

Savannah took in a ragged breath and nodded.

***

Once the two couples were back at the beach house, the women changed into more casual clothes and joined the men on the deck. They were solemnly discussing their experience at Dawna's apartment and taking turns making suppositions as to what happened, when the doorbell rang. Upon opening the door, Savannah greeted two police officers standing on the walkway leading to the small porch.

"Savannah Ivey?" the male officer asked, referring to a small notepad.

"Yes," she said.

"You were a witness to…"

"Well, not exactly a witness," she explained, "…but I was there when they found…the victim…"

He studied her for a moment then said, "I'm Officer Studor." He nodded toward the female officer. "This is Sergeant Markle. We'd like to ask you a few questions."

Savannah stepped back from the door. "Sure. Please come in. Let's sit in here?" she invited, motioning toward the large dining room table. Savannah looked from one to the other of the officers and asked, "So what actually happened?"

"Not sure, yet, but it looks like attempted murder."

"Attempted?" Savannah questioned. When she saw Brianna enter the room from the deck, she said to her, "She's alive."

"Oh, that's good news."

"Are you Brianna?" the officer asked.

She nodded.

"And your last name is…"

"Jordan," she said. "Dr. Brianna Jordan."

"Sis, this is Officer Studor and Sergeant…"

"Markle," the sergeant said.

The officer glanced up at Brianna and then back at his notes. He wrote something on the notepad. "So tell us what happened this evening," he prompted.

Savannah spoke first. "Well, we were coming home from an art show and saw my cat…"

"Your cat?" Sergeant Markle asked, tilting her head.

"Yes," Savannah said. "He escaped somehow and he was outside walking toward the house carrying a shell necklace."

"Wearing a necklace?" Officer Studor asked.

"No, carrying it," Savannah corrected.

"In his mouth?"

Savannah explained. "Yes, it may sound unusual, but it's something he does."

"Like that," Brianna said.

The police officers looked in the direction she pointed and the sergeant said, "Well, look at that. He's carrying something in his mouth…like a dog."

"What is that?" Officer Studor asked, smiling. "A sock?"

"Yes, I think so." Savannah took it from Rags. Holding it up, she said, "One of my daughter's socks."

"So he was carrying a necklace…" Officer Studor prompted.

"Yes, and it appeared to have blood on it. When Peter—that's Peter Whitcomb— remembered that his gallery manager Dawna had recently bought a necklace just like that, he thought maybe it was hers. We got worried when we saw the blood and, since she lives close by, we decided to walk up to her place and…well, they found her and we called you."

"Who walked up there?" the officer asked.

Savannah motioned toward her sister. "Brianna, Peter, his friend, Blake, and I."

"Blake, that's old man Eastman's daughter," the sergeant said to her partner.

Officer Studor continued the questioning. "What did you do or see once you got to…" he referred to his notes again, "…Ms. Paulson's apartment?"

Savannah said, "Well, Peter knocked on the door. There was no answer, so he used a key and he and Blake went inside."

"There was a window wide open with no screen on it," Brianna interjected.

"Did you see the victim?" he asked.

Both Savannah and Brianna shook their head. Savannah said, "No, we just stepped inside the living room. That's all. Only Peter and Blake went in wherever she was."

Officer Studor looked at her and then at Brianna. "Do either of you have anything to add?"

Savannah shook her head. "Just came down from Northern California for a quiet vacation on the beach and landed in the middle of a crime," she lamented.

"How well do you know the victim?" Officer Studor asked.

Savannah explained, "I just met her a few days ago."

When the officer looked at Brianna, she said, "I wouldn't know her from Adam." Then she chuckled.

"What's funny?" he asked, frowning.

"Oh nothing, except that my nephew is here and his name's Adam. That's all." She sat back and scrunched down a little in her chair.

Just then, Rags sauntered into the room again, jumped up on one of the dining room chairs, and stared at the two officers from across the table. "Handsome cat," the sergeant said. "What's his name?"

"Ragsdale," Savannah said.

"Do you always travel with him?"

*Mew*

Everyone looked toward the sound and saw Buffy entering the room from the staircase.

"Gosh, is the baby awake at this time of night?" Savannah asked. "Better go check."

"Uh, just out of curiosity," Sergeant Markle said, "why would you assume the baby's awake just because this cute little cat appears?"

"Oh, she's our babysitter," Savannah explained, before heading out of the room.

The officers looked at Brianna, obviously craving an explanation. Before she could respond, Lexie raced into the room at full speed, sliding across the tile floor as she made the corner into the kitchen; Walter on her tail.

The sergeant chuckled. "Did I just see a cat chasing a dog?"

Before anyone could comment, the pair appeared again. This time the black cat playfully attacked Lexie and coerced her into a wrestling match. Suddenly, Walter scampered off toward the kitchen, Lexie racing after him.

When Brianna noticed the officers looking to her for an explanation, she shrugged. "What can I say? They have some strange animals." The pair still looked puzzled, so Brianna added, "My sister and her husband are both veterinarians…kind of like Dr. and Mrs. Doolittle."

The sergeant suppressed a smile. She took in a deep breath and stood, saying, "Well, I guess that's all we need from you this evening. How long will you be staying?"

"My boyfriend and I are leaving Wednesday and I think my sister's staying for another week or so." Before the officers reached the front door, Brianna said, "Uh-oh."

"What?" Sergeant Markle asked, looking back at her.

She winced and held up a small notepad. "The cat had it," she explained, quietly.

"Huh? Well…I…" Officer Studor stuttered. He patted his shirt pocket before saying, "How'd he...? I mean… where'd he…? That cat?" he asked, pointing.

Just then Michael walked into the room. "Michael," Brianna said. "You'd better teach your cat better manners. He just stole from a policeman."

"Oh no. I'm sorry officers," he said. He then turned and looked at Bud, who had followed him in. "Stop laughing, man, you'll encourage him."

Officer Studor looked at Bud and then Michael. "No harm done." He then nodded in Brianna's direction and said, "Thanks, ma'am for your help."

Brianna couldn't help peering through the wood blinds after the officers left. As she expected, they were both laughing heartily. She grinned and said, "I think we made their day."

She then turned to Michael. "You have quite the conversation piece there in that cat, you know it?"

"Tell me about it," he said, glaring down at Rags.

***

Despite their late night, everyone was up early Sunday morning. They had just finished a leisurely continental breakfast on the deck, when Adam asked Brianna. "Aunt Bri, would you come out and play in the water with me?"

"I'd love to. Can I bring your sister?"

"Sure," he said. "She likes putting her feet in the water."

"I'll walk down with you," Savannah said. "I want to look for more beach glass for my collection."

"How big is your collection?" Brianna asked.

"I have twelve pieces," she said proudly. "…mostly brown and clear."

"The brown ones are from beer bottles," Bud said.

"Yeah, probably. I also have a couple of sea-green pieces, and I'm looking for red and blue."

"Good luck," Brianna said, smirking. "Those are the hardest to find."

Savannah looked at her sister. "How do you know?"

"Mom and I used to pick up beach glass, didn't we, Mom?"

"Sure did. I still have a little box full of it."

Savannah frowned. "Oh, I thought I invented it. You mean other people pick it up, too?"

110

"Yes," Brianna said, laughing. "You thought you were the only one? That's funny."

Before Savannah could comment, Michael walked up and put his arm around her. "Come on, hon, let's go find some beach glass. Coming Gladys?" he invited. "Let's get our feet wet."

They'd been frolicking in the surf for about half an hour when Savannah noticed Peter standing on the deck watching them.

"Hi!" she called out. "Coffee's hot."

He held up the mug in his hand.

Savannah looked back at the others and noticed they were preoccupied on the sand and in the waves, so she slipped into her terry cover-up and joined Peter. "How is she?" she asked.

He stared down at his coffee and said, "It was a close call, Savannah. I almost lost her."

"But she's going to be okay? Does she know who did this? He must have climbed in through that open window. Is that what they think happened?"

Peter walked to a deck chair and slumped as he sat down. "I don't know."

Savannah lowered herself into the chair next to him. "Oh my gosh. Was it someone she knew? She let him into the apartment?"

Peter shook his head and spoke softly. "Could have been, I guess." He hesitated. "She says someone broke in, but things just don't add up." He sat up straight. "They can't find evidence showing that anyone else was there last night." He took a deep breath. "But he could have been wearing gloves, I guess. They want to keep her in the hospital for a few days. She lost a lot of blood."

"What were her injuries?"

"A stab wound—pretty much non-life-threatening—superficial—except she bled for a long time—almost too long."

"Gads," Savannah said, genuinely concerned.

Peter grimaced. "I feel pretty awful. We had a big argument on the phone last night. I was really rough on her. I made accusations. She tried to call me back later, after this…happened…and I didn't pick up. Then I turned my phone off." He looked at Savannah and choked up. "She might have died because I turned my phone off. So your cat really did save her life." He stared down at his coffee for a moment and then asked, "Did you find out how he escaped?"

"No. No one will fess up to letting him out this time. I'm afraid he's discovered his own way out and that's frightening."

"Well, evidently he noticed Dawna's window open and stepped in for a visit. How he found her place is anyone's guess. She says she saw the cat and thought she was dead or hallucinating. She had taken the necklace off just before this…happened. She said she made it into the bathroom to get a washcloth to stop the bleeding. The cat was sitting next to the necklace.  She said she was kind of out of it, but she was sure she saw the cat watching her. He must have picked up the necklace and taken off with it." Peter turned toward Savannah "Now do you suppose he knew it was a clue—that it would bring help—or did he just like the pretty trinket?"

Savannah shook her head. "As a professional in the animal world—you know, from the scientific side—I can't imagine that he has the capacity to reason—to use logic about the things he takes. That concept is too far-fetched. But…" she sighed, "his timing can be incredible."

***

Wednesday morning came much too soon for Brianna. "To think we have to leave today," she complained, as she and Bud sat on the deck with her family, finishing plates of pancakes smothered in strawberries.

Bud wiped his face with a napkin and glanced up at Savannah and Michael. "This has been great. Thanks for including us."

Michael chuckled. "It was interesting seeing Seashore Bud."

Brianna laughed. "Seashore Bud?"

"Yeah, I've seen Cowboy Bud, Veterinarian Bud, Dating Bud, and now Seashore Bud." Michael punched Bud in the arm playfully and said, "Man, you're many-faceted, you know it?"

"Yes, he is," Brianna agreed, grinning.

"So glad you could join us," Savannah said. "It's been loads of fun."

"Sure has," Brianna said. "I loved spending time with my niece and nephew."

"Aunt Bri, when do we have to leave?" Adam asked.

"I think we'd better get on the road by ten. You'll get home kinda late, but your mom said that's okay. You can sleep in the car."

"What time is it now?" he asked.

She looked at her watch. "Eight-thirty."

"Do I have time to do one more beach thing?" he asked.

"Yeah, like what?" Brianna asked.

"Play Frisbee, boogie board, build a castle, swim…"

"Sure," she said. She looked at Michael. "…if it's okay with your dad."

He nodded. "Pick one, Son, and let's go do it."

"Um…I don't know which one I want to do most." he said, appearing to be somewhat overwhelmed.

"Then how about this," Michael said.

Adam perked up. "What?"

"Something we haven't done yet."

"What's that, Dad?"

"Let's go exploring," Michael said, with excitement in his voice. When Adam looked at him inquisitively, Michael continued, "…like pirates. We'll take the binoculars, the magnifying glass, a digging stick, and…oh yes…a goody bag, and we'll hunt for treasure…" he said, giving his voice an eerie quality.

Adam perked up. "Okay!" he shouted. He reached for his dad's hand and pulled him out of the deck chair. "Come on, Dad, let's go. We don't have much time."

Michael slipped into his flip-flops and said with a dramatic flair, "Treasure, ho!" He looked at Adam, who was giggling and shaking his head. "Let's gather our stuff and off we go," Michael said. "Anyone want to join us?"

When no one spoke up, Savannah said, "We'll hold down the fort…uh, batten down the hatches…um, stay aboard ship."

"Have fun!" Brianna called as the explorers stepped off the deck and headed north.

Everyone waved.

An hour later, Michael and Adam returned, their goody bags bulging. "Hey, what did you find?" Brianna called, as Adam stepped up onto the deck smiling broadly.

"Wait 'til you see," he said, excitedly. He ran toward the group and laid his goody bag down. He then proceeded to remove his treasures one by one, sharing a story about each of them. He exhibited a mussel shell he'd removed from a piece of seaweed. He told of finding matching bottle caps far away from each other. He showed a rusty piece of chain that had probably come from a pirate ship anchor. He pulled out sunglasses that had been buried maybe for hundreds of years. And he brought back a heart-shaped rock for Gladys and two pieces of beach glass for Savannah.

"And what did you find?" Savannah asked Michael.

He reached into his bag and pulled out the morning paper and a small box of donut holes.

"Oh, part of the lost scrolls, huh, Michael?" Brianna said.

"And remnants of the Last Supper," Bud joked.

Everyone laughed. Then Brianna said, "Hey, kiddo, go wash the sand off and put on your traveling clothes. We've gotta hit the road."

Adam sighed. "Okay, Aunt Bri," he said, slumping his shoulders.

"Well, I'd better hit the road, too," Gladys said.

"Oh, you're going home?" Brianna asked.

"Just to regroup, make a few calls, and pack some different clothes. I'm tired of wearing the same things. I'll be back later this afternoon."

Once hugs were shared all around and everyone had left, Savannah and Michael took Lily down to the water. "This is the perfect time of day for her to play in the ocean, isn't it? The waves are so small and gentle," Savannah said.

"Yes," Michael agreed, smiling. "She sure gets a kick out of splashing her feet in the water."

Suddenly, the baby began to scream. Michael quickly lifted her up and held her against him while Savannah frantically looked her over. Just about the time she noticed a tiny red spot on the baby's leg, they heard another child nearby call out, "Jellyfish! Jellyfish!"

"Oh no, Michael, I think she was stung. Hurry, let's get her inside. We need to wash the area with vinegar."

"Why do you say that?" he asked, running toward the house with the crying baby.

"I remember it from veterinary school," she said. "But it depends on the type of jellyfish. Did you see that one? What kind was it?"

"I don't know—I think I saw a glob of something that was jelly-like."

"See if you can calm her down," she said. "I'll look for vinegar in the kitchen."

"Aw, does that feel better, sweetheart?" Michael crooned, as Savannah smoothed a vinegar-soaked rag over the baby's leg. She then ran her hand over Lily's head. "Yes, that seemed to help with the sting. But now she's sleepy. I'm worried, Michael. I think we should take her to the emergency room."

"Where's the hospital?"

"I don't know. We can use the GPS," she said. "I'll get a blanket and throw on some clothes." She started to leave the room, then turned and said, "I'll bring you a shirt, Michael."

Upon their arrival at the emergency room, Savannah told the receptionist they thought Lily had been stung by a jellyfish and insisted that she ask someone if it was okay for the baby to go to sleep. "If we have to wait, I know she'll fall asleep," she said. "We need to know if it's okay."

The large Hispanic woman returned to her post within a minute or two and assured Savannah and Michael that it would be perfectly okay if Lily went to sleep. "The doctor will see you shortly," she said, as the couple went in search of a suitable place to sit in the sparsely occupied waiting room.

Forty-five minutes later, the doctor finished his examination and explained gently, "Well, now, no harm done. The jellyfish we see this time of year have a painful sting, but they're harmless as far as any damaging effects."

"It was okay if she went to sleep, then?" Savannah asked.

"Yes," he said. "She's probably exhausted after the ordeal. And you must be too, Mom and Dad," he said with a chuckle. "Your little girl is just fine. Take her home and let her sleep as long as she wants. And you might get her a little swimming pool to put on the sand, then she won't come in contact with any more jellyfish."

"Good idea, doc," Michael said, shaking the man's hand. "Thanks so much."

On their way home, Savannah, who sat next to Lily in the backseat, her hand on the baby's leg, gazed lazily out the car window when something caught her attention. "Hey, isn't that Kara?" she asked.

Michael squinted in the direction she pointed. "Yes, looks like she's carrying one of Peter's paintings." On a whim, he pulled the car over, rolled the window down, and called out, "Hey Kara, you look lost."

Once the young woman recognized Savannah and Michael, she walked up to the car and peered in. "Hi," she said, addressing them both. "Yes, I kinda am lost. I'm supposed to deliver this painting and I can't find the address. These apartment buildings are so confusing. I've called Dawna twice for directions and I still can't find it."

"So Dawna's back to work?" Savannah asked.

Kara nodded. "Seems fine to me, except she's bossier than usual," she said, wrinkling her nose.

"How's that?" Michael asked.

"Well, I showed up at the gallery for my shift around ten and she sent me right out to run a bunch of errands; all I have left to do is deliver this painting. Last time I called her, I told her I have a class soon and, the way things were going, I might not have time to make the delivery. You know what she said? She told me to just take the painting home if I can't find the buyer. Now that's odd, don't you think?"

"Yeah, it kinda is," Savannah agreed.

"Where's Peter today? Does he know the customer?" Michael asked.

"He had to fly up north to talk to some executives about a show. He'll be back this evening, I think. I didn't want to bother him about this."

"Can we give you a ride somewhere?" Michael offered.

"No thanks. My car's around the block there." She looked at her watch and said, "Hey, maybe you could take this back to the gallery since you're going that way."

"Sure, no problem," Savannah said from the backseat. She opened the car door so Kara could slide the painting in next to her.

Kara smiled at the couple. "Thanks so much. Now I'll have time for lunch before school," she said, waving as they drove away from the curb.

Michael glanced at Savannah in the rearview mirror. "I think I'll drop it off before we go home, if that's okay with you."

Savannah nodded, then said, "Michael, you know, seeing Kara reminded me of something."

"What?" he asked.

"Remember when we were at the mansion for the art show?"

"Yeah."

"Well, I saw her and Charlynn there."

"You did? I didn't see them." He thought for a moment. "But there were a lot of people and a lot of activities all over that property."

"Yes, there were." She swooned. "What an evening that was. But yeah, while we were listening to the harpist, I saw them at a distance. They were hiding and doing something to what looked like a painting."

"Really?" Michael asked, frowning into the mirror at her. "Like what?"

"I'm not sure, but they were having fun doing it. They were laughing." She thought for a moment and then said, "Michael, it looked like they were destroying a painting. But why would they do that? It doesn't make sense…unless…"

Just then, Michael pulled into a parking space near the gallery and asked, "Do you want to come in with me?"

"No. Go on in, I'll wait here with Lily."

"Hi, Dawna," Michael said, entering the gallery. "Brought you something."

Dawna spun around quickly and appeared stunned when she saw Michael. "Uh, what?" she stammered. "You know Peter's not in today. He's out of town," she said, taking Michael's arm and ushering him back toward the exit.

He turned to face her and held up the painting. "We ran into Kara. She couldn't find the address for this customer and we told her we'd…"

"Oh that's great. Thanks, Michael," she said, taking the painting in both of her hands and holding it in front of her.

Michael stood there for a moment. He glanced around the gallery, then said, "Sure. 'Bye," before walking out.

"That was quick," Savannah said, when he returned.

He climbed into the car and sat there for a moment. "Well, if that wasn't strange."

"Is she okay?" Savannah asked.

He turned and looked back at Savannah. "Yeah, seems healthy. But she sure wanted me out of there in a hurry."

"Michael, she doesn't know us very well. She's probably more interested in customers who are in a buying mood."

"Well, you want to buy one—remember?" he said

"Sure do."

"Why not now? Go buy that painting, Savannah. Something's not right in there. It looks different."

"Ooh, Michael," Savannah complained. "I'm tired. I just want to get our baby home and I'd like to take a nap—maybe in a lounge chair. Please, can't we just go home?"

Michael glanced back at the gallery and shook his head. "Yeah, I don't blame you. Sure, we can go home. Probably my imagination, anyway."

**Chapter 4**

That night, after Lily was asleep, Savannah and Michael were enjoying a balmy evening on the deck, each with a glass of wine. "What a nice week," she said. "I really enjoyed having quality time with Bri and my mom, Adam, and all the activities with Peter and his friends." She held up her glass toward the moonlight. "Only I miss…"

"What do you miss?" Michael asked, rolling toward her in the chaise lounge they shared.

"My pretty wine glasses Auntie gave us for a wedding gift," she said.

"Oh, you're silly. I would drink out of recycled dog-food cans to enjoy this week with you."

She pulled back and looked at him. "Recycled dog-food cans? Ewww." She laughed and added, "We could manage that, you know."

Lexie raised her head and Savannah petted her. She then turned toward Michael and sighed. "This is so nice," she said, snuggling against him. He responded by kissing her and saying, "Mmm, it sure is."

He then stiffened and groaned. "Damn, my phone." He looked at the screen. "It's a text." Straining to read it, he said, "Peter wonders if we're decent. Wants to join us."

"Now?" Savannah whined. "Yeah, sure I guess," she said, lifting herself up on one elbow. "Tell him to come on out."After Michael ended the call, she said, "I'm comfy, you move."

"No you move. I'm comfy," he teased.

She nudged him with her hands. "Go, Michael."

"Okaaayyy," he said, pretending to pout. He ran his hand through his hair as he stood and then took another lounge chair next to Savannah's.

She sat up, straightened her shorts and t-shirt, then raised the back on the chaise lounge. She looked at Michael, smiled, and winked. "I love you," she said.

"Me, too," Michael said, reaching out and squeezing her hand.

Just then, Peter stepped up onto the deck. "Hi, you two."

"Oh, hi," Savannah said. "I expected you to come through the house."

"Naw, I came down the back stairs with the dog. Okay if she joins us?"

"Sure," Michael said. "Come on Sakari," he encouraged.

Savannah and Michael smiled as they watched her wriggle toward them. Suddenly, Lexie noticed the husky-mix and greeted her. The two dogs circled one another, attempting to take in each other's scent. Once the introduction ritual was completed, the dogs found their separate comfort zones and both laid down.

"Would you like red wine or white?" Savanna asked. "Or we have beer."

"Whatever you're having is fine," he said. "Want me to get it?"

"No, I'm on my way. Gonna check on the baby."

"I thought that's what the monitor was for," Peter said.

"Well, we had a trip to the emergency room with her today, so we're keeping a closer eye on her," Michael explained, rather solemnly.

"What happened?" Peter asked, looking from one to the other.

"Jellyfish sting," Michael answered, as Savannah entered the house.

"Oh, those things hurt," Peter said. "Is she all right?"

"Sure. We took her to emergency because she seemed to be so upset and we didn't know what we were dealing with." He choked up. "Some of those things are deadly, you know."

"Yes, I know. But we don't get those around here much, if at all."

"Could have saved a lot of trouble and strife, not to mention money, if I'd known that," Michael said.

"Well, glad to know she's okay," Peter said.

Michael chuckled. "Yeah, she's better than her over-reactive parents."

Peter sat quietly for a moment, then said, "You're a lucky man, Michael."

"Don't I know it," he said in all seriousness.

"So tell me; where did you find this fabulous woman?"

Michael chuckled. "She came into the clinic one day with her spunky aunt to pick up a couple of kittens. Her aunt had been clobbered with a rock that day and needed some help, but I couldn't keep my eyes off her beautiful niece. It took a while to convince her to marry me, but she finally said yes and…yeah, man, life is great."

"Moscato, it is," Savannah said when she returned. She handed Peter the glass and then looked from one to the other of the men, who were both staring at her. "What?"

"Nothing," Michael said. "How's Lily?"

"Just fine. Sleeping like a baby, and so is Buffy."

"Where's the big boy?" Peter asked, grinning. "Has he been in any trouble, lately?"

"He's out of the doghouse for now," she said. "Just saw him sprawled in one of Buffy's foo-foo beds."

"That cat's too much," he said. "He's a comedian."

"Yeah, he's pretty funny. But when he's your responsibility, you sometimes lose your sense of humor," she said. "Right Michael?"

"You got that right," he said. "Hey, Peter, we stopped by your gallery today."

Savannah interjected. "Oh yes, we had to rescue Kara."

Peter looked confused. He glanced from one to the other of them. "What happened?" he asked.

"Well, Kara was trying to deliver a painting downtown not too far from the hospital and couldn't find the address," Savannah explained. "Poor thing had been walking all over the place with this big painting."

"What?" Peter asked. "I wonder where she was taking it. I don't know of anyone who asked for delivery in that area." He ran his hand through his hair. "But maybe the order came in while I was gone." He looked at Savannah. "So did she find the address?"

"No. She was going to be late for a class, so we took the painting back to your gallery."

"That's odd. Didn't she check the address with Dawna?"

Michael nodded. "Yes. She said she had been in touch with her and Dawna would give her different directions and she got confused."

"Strange," Peter said. "Very strange."

"But here's something else odd," Michael said, leaning forward, cupping his wine glass in both hands. "I took the painting in to Dawna and she practically threw me out of the gallery."

Peter scowled. "What? Why would she do that?"

Michael shrugged. "You got me. Maybe she was expecting customers or I was interrupting her lunch or…

heck I don't know. But she sure seemed to want me out of there quick."

Peter sat quietly for a few moments, peering into his wine glass.

Finally Michael broke the silence by saying, "There was something else odd, Peter." He hesitated. "Things in your gallery looked different." Sounding apologetic, he said, "It could be me, but I thought things had been moved around. Something was different in there."

Peter thought about that for a moment and then said, "Well, I guess Dawna could have exhibited the art differently today. When she's not busy, she will sometimes move things around. But I don't think it would be so dramatic as to be noticeable." He shook his head. "Although maybe she had a lot of time on her hands because it was another really slow day." He lowered his eyes and let out a sigh. "Sales were down, again."

"So where'd you go today?" Savannah asked, in an attempt to lighten the mood. "Did you fly off somewhere exotic?"

"Yeah, but I didn't get to enjoy the benefits."

Savannah and Michael waited for Peter's explanation. Finally, he said, "I took a commuter jet to Frisco and met with the board of a prestigious art show. Evidently, someone had convinced them they should reject my application."

Savannah frowned. "Gads, is that the type of thing that comes with fame, Peter?"

He shook his head slowly. "I don't know. I just don't know."

"So what about those cameras you wanted installed?" Michael asked. "We've been so busy vacationing that we haven't talked about it again."

"Been thinking on it." He looked Michael in the eyes. "You brought up some good points about using them in the gallery. I mean, the gallery is so broken up—we'd need a lot of cameras. I'm wondering if a recording device would be better for my purposes."

"Hmmm, and put that where? You'd end up with the same problem. Just what do you think you're going to discover through cameras or recordings?" Michael asked.

"Good question." Peter thinned his lips. "I want to know who's causing the problems in my connections…why I'm not making the sales I usually do…who's vandalizing and taking my paintings. Savannah found that one that had been tossed in a Dumpster, for heaven's sake. Who is doing all of this? Is it another artist—someone I know well and trust in my gallery and studio? Is it an employee—Kara, Dawna, Charlynn, or someone from the janitorial service? Maybe it's my technology gal who sets up my slide shows and keeps my website updated.  Or is it someone who's close to one of the employees, or a beach bum who feels I snubbed him or who's jealous because he's limited to selling his own art on the sly out on the beach?"

"Maybe it's an old girlfriend," Savannah offered. "Or a former employee."

Peter looked at her. "I just don't know. I threw a bum out of the gallery a month or so ago. I roughed him up some and he was enraged. Could be that he's messing with me."

"What did he do?" Michael asked.

"Oh, he was scaring my customers—talking about how my paintings were of the devil or something. He got pretty obnoxious."

"What did that guy look like?" Savannah asked, sitting on the edge of her chair.

"Oh, greying, long hair, beard, baggy clothes."

"Grey, huh?"

"Yeah, why?" Peter asked.

She frowned. "I thought it might be the guy I've seen hanging around your gallery. But he has brown hair and beard. No grey, that I noticed."

"It's the beach," he said. "California beaches are prime spots for the homeless and the bums. Your description fits about a quarter of that population and mine fits another quarter."

"So was it a successful trip?" Savannah asked. Peter sat straighter and smiled. "Actually, yes…in more ways than one." When it appeared that the others were waiting for an explanation, he said, "I met someone on the plane."

"Don't tell me," Michael said.

"What?" Peter asked, smirking a little.

"A woman, right? A beautiful woman."

"What can I say?" Peter said, laughing.

"So what will you hire her to do for you?" Michael asked. "…shine your shoes, walk your dog, iron your sheets?"

"She's a psychic," he said, quietly.

"A what?" Michael asked.

"A psychic. And she's good, too." He looked at the couple. "Hey, I invited her over tomorrow night. I thought I'd cater a meal. Would love it if you'd join us." Before they could respond, Peter said, "You know, she told me some things. She guessed…or she read my freckles or something…and knew that I was distressed."

"Heck, I could tell that the minute you walked in tonight," Michael said. "She's probably good at reading body language."

"Naw, it's more than that," Peter defended. "Rochelle told me I had changed careers. Now who would know that?"

"Good guess. Most people change careers these days—more than once," Michael reasoned.

Peter took a sip of wine and gazed at Michael over his glass. He said more quietly. "She picked up on the fact that someone's after me. Said to protect my art because she sees it being destroyed. Destroyed!" he repeated.

"What do you think that means?" Michael asked, pouring himself more wine. "Fire? Flood? A Mother Nature thing?"

"Or something otherworldly?" Savannah suggested.

"Like what?" Peter asked, chuckling. "Ghosts making them disappear? A witch casting a spell? Gremlins beaming them up to Pluto?"

Everyone laughed. Then Peter turned sullen. "I don't actually know what it means. She wasn't specific. If she saw what would destroy them, she didn't reveal it," he said. He was quiet for a moment and then said, "How about a late dinner out here? It's supposed to be nice again."

Savannah looked hopefully at Michael. "Sounds wonderful. Okay with you, Michael?"

"Sure," he nodded. "I wouldn't mind dining with a psychic."

***

Thursday night, just after seven, the doorbell rang.

"Come in," Michael invited, opening the front door for Peter and Rochelle. Savannah promptly joined them in the living room.

"Savannah and Michael Ivey, this is Rochelle," Peter said.

The woman smiled and offered her hand to Michael and then Savannah. "Nice to meet you. Peter has told me… quite a bit about you."

"Aw, Peter," Michael said, "you haven't been making up outrageous stories again, have you?"

"Nope," he said, grinning. "Only the truth shall pass through these lips."

"Well, we've heard some good things about you, too, Rochelle," Savannah said, smiling.

Just then, she noticed Gladys walk in from the kitchen, carrying the baby. "Oh, Rochelle, this is my mom Gladys and, this week, our nanny." She kissed the baby on the cheek. "This is our daughter, Lily."

"What a sweet child," Rochelle gushed, walking toward her. "How old is she?" she asked, reaching out and taking the baby's hand.

"Six months," Savannah said, smiling.

Rochelle glanced at Gladys. "You must be a proud grandmother."

Gladys nodded and looked down at Lily. "Oh yes," she said, smiling.

Rochelle made brief eye contact with Savannah and then studied Lily's face. "She knows stuff, this one," she said. She stood straight, barely taller than Gladys's five-five-inch height.

"Knows stuff?" Michael repeated.

"Yes, she's still tuned in to the other side. She has that…deep understanding that some children have. Most who do, soon forget." Rochelle brushed her light-brown side bangs to one side before saying, "Encourage her when she talks about things you may not understand—imaginary friends, a family member who has passed, dreams…things like that."

"Uh, okay," Michael said. "She hasn't done much talking yet…but…"

"Oh, Michael…" Savannah said, scolding. She then addressed Rochelle. "That's fascinating. I'll definitely listen for things like that when she starts talking to us."

Gladys looked from one couple to the other, shook her head, and said, "Well, it's getting late. I think I'll put this wonder-child to bed. Have fun, kids," she called over her shoulder as she headed for the stairs.

"Want me to carry her up, Gladys?" Michael asked.

"No, I'm okay. Thanks."

"Wait," Savannah said. She walked over and hugged the baby. "Night-night, precious."

Michael kissed the side of Lily's head. "Sleep tight, baby girl."

"Too bad she isn't loved, isn't it?" Peter said, laughing.

Rochelle eyes followed Gladys and the baby. "She is a dear child."

"Can I get anyone a glass of wine, beer, champagne?" Michael offered. "We have a sweet white, a dry white, and sangria. Savannah made the sangria."

"Oh, sangria sounds lovely," Rochelle said, "Thank you."

Peter agreed. "Me, too."

Rochelle glanced toward the kitchen door. "Oh, look at this," she said. "I thought I felt kitty energy in the house."

Savannah turned in the direction she pointed. "That's Buffy. She's our little sweetheart."

Rochelle asked, "Can I pick her up?"

"Sure," Savannah said, "only…"

"Only what?" she asked, raising her eyebrows.

"Well, she stays pretty close to the baby, so she may not want to be held right now."

"Hey, Gladys, come back," Michael called.

"What?" she said, returning to the top of the stairs.

"Just wait for a moment, would you? Rochelle wants to meet Buffy. If you take the baby away, she'll follow you."

Gladys laughed. "She does like being with Lillianna."

Savannah nodded. "Yup, she's like her guardian angel."

Rochelle walked toward the little Himalayan-mix cat and lifted her. "She's so light. I thought she'd be heavier. I guess she's mostly fur." She snuggled with the cat and then looked up at the others. "She's purring. She is just yummy. What a gentle soul."

Savannah smiled, tilted her head, and asked, "Rochelle, would you like to watch Lily's and Buffy's bedtime ritual?"

"Sure," Rochelle said, looking a little puzzled.

"Come on," she invited.

Savannah and Rochelle met Gladys at the top of the stairs and followed her into the little alcove where Lily's portable crib was set up. "Oh, that must be Buffy's bed," Rochelle said, looking down at the pink canopy bed. "How cute is that?" She cocked her head. "But it's occupied. Now who's this?" she asked, seeing Rags sprawled across the bed.

"Oh Rags, you know that's Buffy's bed," Savannah scolded. "Go get in the other one."

She lifted Rags out of the bed and Rochelle put Buffy down on the floor near it. The little Himmie-mix promptly climbed into the bed and sat down, watching the activity around her.

Savannah explained, "Now, as soon as Lily goes to bed, Buffy will curl up and go to sleep. When Lily wakes up in the morning or if she wakes up in the night, Buffy comes to tell us." She laughed. "She's better than that baby monitor we bought."

"Food's here," Michael called from the bottom of the stairs.

"Well, goodnight Buffy and baby Lily," Savannah said. "Thanks Mom."

"Nice meeting all of you, Gladys, Lily, Buffy, and… Ralph?" Rochelle questioned.

Savannah laughed. "Rags," she corrected.

Once the gals had caught up with the guys in the living room, Peter said, "Ladies, please come out on the deck and be seated. We'll serve your dinner."

"Well, how cool is that?" Savannah said. "Come on Rochelle, we've set up a cozy table for four."

"Nice," Rochelle said, approaching the beautifully set table. She noticed the cluster of enclosed candles flickering in the center of it and lining the deck railings. "It's lovely."

After the salads and bread were served and the couples had engaged in table-talk for a while, Rochelle suddenly asked, "What's that?" She looked to her right and said, "Oh, it's him…what did you say his name is?"

Savannah followed Rochelle's gaze and spotted Rags sitting on the back of an overstuffed chair in the living room, peering out at them. "Rags."

"Or Ragsie," Michael said, teasing Savannah.

"Well, he's my first baby," she defended.

"Was that always his name?" Rochelle asked. "It doesn't seem to fit him just right."

Savannah's eyes widened. "Wow!" she said. "I haven't thought about that in years, but yeah, he did have a different name when I adopted him. At the shelter, they were calling him…"

Rochelle put her hand up and said, "Let me guess. What comes to me when I look at him is Tucker or Tank…" She peered at Savannah through narrowed eyes and added, "Toby?"

Savannah laughed. "Awfully close. It was Tonka."

"Why did you change it?" she asked.

"I don't know. I guess I thought he should have a more sophisticated name."

"Rags?" she asked, lowering her brow.

"Well, it's Ragsdale," Savannah said.

"Ooh," Rochelle said. "So an interesting name for an interesting cat." She gazed at him for a few moments and then said, "He's…special." Savannah and Michael watched Rochelle as she spoke. When she broke her gaze with Rags, she looked at Savannah and then Michael and said, "He's an unusual cat. Not ordinary." She paused, waiting for an explanation.

"Well…" Savannah started.

"He's a thief," Peter blurted, laughing.

Savannah shrugged. "That about sums it up."

"Oh," Rochelle said, a knowing smile on her face, "a klepto cat."

"Yes," Michael said, "and he works with our local police department."

Rochelle's eyes widened. She smiled. "Of course he does."

"Do you have pets?" Savannah asked.

"I do," Rochelle said, blotting her lips with her napkin. She laid it in her lap and continued, "I have a pair

of Siamese. They're brother and sister and as different as…
well, your Buffy and Ragsdale. Like most cats, they know
things…" she laughed. "…or they give the impression that
they do, but neither of them has that deep…I don't know…
knowingness that Ragsdale seems to have."

Michael and Savannah looked at each other. She
said, "Fascinating. He has been involved in some off-the-
wall things. But you really think he…knows stuff? That's
kind of spooky."

"Oh no, no," Rochelle said, shaking her head. "Not
spooky. He needs to be appreciated for all that he brings to
the table."

Michael chuckled. "Yeah, he brings a lot to the
table—guests' wallets, prescription medications, private
mail, Savannah's underwear…Peter's right; he's a thief."

"He's highly curious; very social, right?"

Savannah and Michael nodded.

Rochelle continued, "And he's clever. He's smart.
Honor that."

"Interesting that you picked up on all that just by
looking at him."

"It's in his eyes. They tell a lot."

The other three stared at the cat.

"Rochelle, so tell us, do you have clients?"
Savannah asked.

"I have some clients. Mainly, I use my abilities for
the good of the people I meet, if you know what I mean."

Michael and Savannah waited to hear more.

"My passion is working with autistic children."

"Oh really?" Savannah asked.

"Yes, these are really special kids. I believe many
of them are highly intelligent and they've come into this
world with a spiritual awareness not normally available to

most children—a connection that continues for most of them throughout their lives, if they're given the opportunity to embrace it. It's just all really intriguing," she said.

Savannah took a sip of sangria. "Sounds like it. I'd love to know more."

"Ready for your entree?" Peter asked, breaking in.

"Oh yes," Savannah said, standing and reaching for the salad plates.

"Sit, my dear," Michael said, taking two plates from her hands. "We're your servers tonight, right Peter?"

"Absolutely," Peter said, picking up the other two salad plates. "Seafood platters coming up."

"Yum," Savannah replied. Once the men had left the room, she leaned toward Rochelle. "You really are a fascinating woman. How did you get involved in such a rich lifestyle?"

"Oh," she said, as if a bit taken aback, "I was born with…some abilities, it seems, and my grandmother encouraged them. She lived with us throughout most of my life. My brother was born when I was seven. He was later diagnosed as autistic. In my childhood innocence, I could relate to him when no one else could. We were kind of on the same plane—a spiritual plane, if you will. When Brian died with my mother in a car accident, I felt such a deep hole in my heart and in my life. One day it came to me that I might be able to fill that hole by working with people like Brian. I'm so glad I followed my intuition."

"So you fulfill your spiritual side through your work within the spiritual realm. Cool," Savannah said.

She laughed. "You've pretty much nailed me, Savannah. Good job." She looked at Savannah. "You and Michael are wonderful together."

"I know," she said. "I can't imagine not sharing this life together."

Rochelle smiled and reached for Savannah's hand. She took it, closed her eyes and said, "You were destined to be together. You have a long and happy life together. Just keep loving each other and your children."

"Children?" Michael said when he and Peter returned.

Rochelle looked at him inquisitively. "I'm seeing more than one child. One has dark hair." She looked at Michael. "Like you. A boy."

"Yes, my son, Adam." He smiled. "Hey, you're good."

"Just wide open," she said. "I let it all come in. I've learned to not filter it so much."

Peter and Michael placed large platters of scallops, shrimp, crab, and lobster in front of the women and then at their own places.

"Looks wonderful," Savannah said.

"Sure does," Rochelle agreed. As she picked up her fork, she said, "There are more children, by the way,"

Michael had taken a bite of crab. He glanced up at Rochelle, looked at Savannah, and said, with his mouth full, "for us?" pointing his fork between himself and Savannah.

Rochelle nodded "Yup," she said, smiling.

"Yes!" Michael said, pumping the air with his fist. Savannah grinned and the two of them leaned toward each other and kissed.

"You made their day," Peter said.

Rochelle smiled. "I love when that happens. It's refreshing to meet someone with such a lovely quality about their relationship."

"And then there's me," Peter said sullenly, smirking.

"Don't be so hard on yourself, Peter. You just must be careful—play it smart. You'll be okay. But do as I say and protect your work, will you?" She took a bite of shrimp and then a sip of sangria. "Peter, I have more to tell you, but let's wait until after dinner, okay? I want to concentrate on this wonderful meal."

He nodded, his eyes glistening in the candlelight. "Glad you like it."

After a while, Rochelle said, "He wants out."

Savannah looked up from her meal. "Huh? Oh, Rags? Yes, he does. Loves to be out."

"Do you let him out?" she asked.

"Sure, but with restrictions. He has been known to escape. He's done it three times since we've been here. That's frightening."

"Why?" she asked.

"Well, I'm afraid he'll get lost or injured or someone will pick him up."

"He's not," she said.

"What?" Savannah cocked her head.

"He's not afraid. He's one confident dude. Knows where he's going and why."

"Really?" Michael said. "Well, you did say he knows stuff."

"Yes. Can he come out here? I'd like to share his space."

Michael and Savannah looked at each other. He suggested, "How about after dinner. He may attack our plates with all of this good seafood on it."

After a few minutes, Michael pushed away from the table. "I'm stuffed. That was something special, Peter. Thank you."

"The experience isn't over yet," Peter said, mysteriously.

"What more could there be?" Savannah asked. "I couldn't eat another bite."

"Even dark chocolate mousse with espresso whipped cream?" he asked, enticingly.

Savannah swooned. "Oh, Peter, you sure know how to tempt a woman."

"Doesn't he?" Rochelle agreed. "Sounds luscious." She picked up her spoon. "Bring it on," she said.

Everyone laughed.

"Coffee, anyone?" Michael asked.

"Sure," Savannah said.

"Yes," Rochelle agreed.

"Delicious," Savannah said after devouring most of her dessert. When she noticed that everyone else had finished, she said, "Here, I'll carry in the dishes and bring Rags out for a visit."

"Never mind," Michael said. "Remember, it's the guys' turn to impress."

Savannah winked at him. "Well, I'm certainly impressed."

"Keep this up," Rochelle quipped, "and I won't be able to button my dress."

"It's a darling dress," Savannah said. "Looks comfortable, but elegant—my kind of wardrobe."

Rochelle laughed. "I made it years ago."

"You sew, too?" Savannah asked.

"I used to. It was my creative outlet of choice. Now I do photography. Love photography."

"Really?" Savannah leaned toward her. "What do you shoot?"

"I enjoy photographing wildlife in their habitat—you know, birds, squirrels—I have this great shot of a fox I took out at the Channel Islands."

"Cool," Savannah said. "I can see how photography could fulfill your creative urges. It's something I enjoy, too, but haven't had much time to pursue it with any gusto."

"Well, hello Ragsdale," Rochelle said when he walked up to her upon being released—on his leash—from the house. "You're quite a handsome cat, aren't you?" she said, petting him and scratching him around the neck. He stood up and put his paws on her lap. She ran her hand gently over his paws. "A cat that allows you to touch his paws is a trusting cat. Cats that trust are either intelligent or they haven't learned to be cautious."

"Interesting," Savannah said. "Hey, I'd like to move around a bit—work some of this meal off. It's so bright out tonight, we could walk on the beach—anyone game?"

*Meow*, Rags said, jumping down from Rochelle's lap.

"How many words does he understand?" Rochelle asked.

"Oh, uh, well, I don't know, but he does seem to know 'walk' and 'outside.'"

"Let's go," Peter said. "Wait, I'll get a flashlight."

After they'd walked for a while in the gentle surf, Rags darting in and out among their feet and even getting his paws wet a time or two, Peter said, "So, Rochelle, you said you have some suggestions for me."

She took his arm and began walking alongside him as Savannah and Michael strolled hand-in-hand ahead of them with Rags.

"Peter, Peter, Peter," she said.

He winced. "Oh, this doesn't sound good."

"You're a wonderfully talented man. You even have more of a business head than most artists—anyway that's my sense. Am I right?"

"Probably, I guess," he said, shrugging. He looked down at her and noticed her soft brown hair blowing in the breeze around her pretty face. "Do I sense a great big 'but' coming?"

She laughed. "You do. You're sensitive, Peter. You know that, don't you?"

"Uh, well…"

"Well, you are. You could be so much more successful in your relationships—and I mean business as well as personal—if only you would…"

"Would what?" he asked, eager to know more.

"Well, if you'd listen and believe what you hear."

"Listen to…what? My business associates, my customers?"

Rochelle laughed. "No. Absolutely not. That's what you should *not* be doing. No, Peter," she said, facing him, "to you," she said, pushing her finger into his chest. "Listen to your inner voice."

When Peter glanced up and noticed that Savannah and Michael had walked several yards ahead with the cat, he looked into Rochelle's striking brown eyes, bent down, and kissed her gently. When he pulled away, he said, rather breathlessly, "I'd apologize for that, but a little voice told me to do it."

Rochelle broke out laughing. "Good for you, Peter," she said. "I do believe you're starting to get it. Yes!" she said loudly. She glanced ahead and saw that Michael and Savannah were engaged in their own quiet conversation, and she said, "My inner voice was saying the same thing." She eased one hand around the back of his neck, pulled him to her, and kissed him back." She then slid her arm through his and they resumed walking. "This is such a lovely evening. And you have wonderful friends. Thank you for including me, Peter."

"You're welcome." They walked in silence for a moment and then he said, "I'd like to see you again,"

"I'd like that, too." She looked up at him for a few moments. "Now, Peter, back to business. Be careful who you trust, will you? And protect those paintings of yours. They are a target." She shook her head. "I don't know why or how or who, but I see them at risk of destruction."

They had just caught up with Savannah and Michael, who heard Rochelle's prediction. "Gosh, that's dire," Michael said. He addressed Peter. "Would it be possible to remove them from your gallery and put them in hiding someplace?"

"I can't close the gallery," he said.

"Yeah, if you close it, you won't ever get a bead on who's doing this to you," Savannah reasoned.

"Can you remove your best work; your newer pieces…?" Michael asked.

"And the one I want to buy," Savannah added.

"Yes, and replace them with…maybe your prints and some of your earlier works that aren't as good," Michael suggested.

"Aren't as good?" Peter said, as if insulted. "They're all good, Michael, or they wouldn't be in the gallery."

"Oh, of course. Sorry, buddy."

"Michael's right," Rochelle said. "That's exactly what I'd do." Everyone was quiet for a moment, caught up in their own thoughts and the ocean sounds, when Rochelle said, "Be careful of the women who surround you."

"What?" Peter asked.

"Peter, I thought about this and analyzed it before saying it. I'm obviously attracted to you, so I wanted to make sure my heart wasn't driving this thought. I had to be clear…know that it was valid. It is. I sense negative vibes with regard to at least one of the women around you. She could bring you down, Peter."

Everyone was silent while Peter digested that last comment. And then Rochelle said, "I'd like to see your gallery sometime."

He nodded and cleared his throat. "How about now? It's a block away from here."

"Okay." She looked at the cat. "Are sandy feet and cats allowed?"

"After hours, anything goes," he quipped.

"Nice location," Rochelle said, as they approached the gallery. She looked at the building. "Quaint and cute. Has a sense of professionalism, that's for sure."

"Are you getting all of that from your inner voice?" Peter asked, as he inserted his key into the door lock.

"No, I used to be in advertising, until I realized how phony it is," she replied.

Everyone laughed.

When the door opened, Peter walked over to shut off the alarm. "That's not right," he said.

"What?" Michael asked.

Peter sighed deeply and scowled. "The alarm wasn't set." He turned on the lights. "Anyone here?" he called.

Just then they heard what sounded like a door slamming. "What was that?" Peter asked. He motioned for the women to wait near the front door. "Is anyone here?" he called out again. He and Michael looked at each other and then the two of them walked toward the back of the gallery and disappeared.

In a couple of minutes they returned. "Damn," Peter said. "I think someone was here and they slipped out through the back door. I'd better look around and see if they took anything." He scanned the room with his eyes. "Things seem to be in order. I see where a couple of paintings have been replaced, but those probably sold and one of the gals hung these in their place."

"Do you keep money here, Peter?" Michael asked.

"A little, sometimes. Depends on if we've had a chance to go to the bank." He headed for the office and opened a desk drawer. Michael followed close behind. "The petty cash is here," Peter observed, "and it looks like a bank deposit ready to go. Wait," he said, "this is Dawna's deposit. That's odd. Why would she bring her deposit to work?" He shrugged. "Oh well, her personal business, I guess." He started to put it back and then added, "That's a lot of checks. I wonder where she got them."

In the meantime, while Rochelle walked through the gallery admiring Peter's work, Savannah stood in place, holding Rags's leash and looking around the main gallery. Suddenly, she felt a tug on the leash. "No, no, Rags. Where do you think you're going?" she said, hurrying to follow him.

"What's he doing?" Michael asked, when he and Peter returned to the main gallery.

"He walked behind that painting and knocked it over," she said.

"Well, why isn't it hanging?" Peter asked. "It shouldn't be just leaning up against the panel like that." He started to reach for it, but Savannah said, "Wait a minute—

this isn't your work, is it, Peter?" She stepped back, peering at it suspiciously. "There's something different about it."

Peter scrutinized the painting. "Oh, my God. No, that's not mine."

Michael peered at it from behind Savannah. "Where do you think it came from?"

"Something wrong?" Rochelle asked, joining the others.

Peter shook his head. "Naw, probably not." He turned to Savannah and Michael. "Artists often bring their paintings in for my evaluation. Someone probably left it with Dawna or Kara. I'll check with them tomorrow." He looked at the painting again and said, as if to himself, "It sure is a pretty good copy of *my* work." He then noticed Rochelle standing near him and he asked, "So did you tour the place?"

"Yes. I could spend a whole day in here. Your art is wonderful, and it certainly validates my sense of you. I especially love seeing the playful aspect. Really delightful," she said. "I can see your dark side, but it's overcome by light." She turned to him. "Yes, I like Peter the artist as much as Peter the individual."

"Well, thank you," he said, bowing deeply. He looked at his watch. "Hey, six a.m. comes early. I don't know about the rest of you, but I'd better get some sleep. I'll lock up and set the alarm and let's hoof it back home, shall we?"

Just then Rags darted in front of Savannah. "Oops, careful Ragsie. You're gonna trip me."

"Here, I'll take him," Michael offered.

Savannah handed him the leash. "Do you think you should call the police about the break-in?" she asked Peter as she walked toward the front door alongside Rochelle.

Peter stopped and looked down at the key in his hand and then back into the gallery. "I don't know. Nothing was taken and I suspect one of the gals left the door open. Let's just go," he said, taking a few steps toward the alarm panel.

"Come on, big guy. Time to go," Michael said. "What are you doing?" he asked.

Everyone turned to see Rags staring at a painting hung low on one of the panels. Michael started to pick him up when Savannah said, "Wait. Give me your phone, Michael. I want to get a picture. That's cute. He's just sitting there staring at that painting like some sort of art critic."

Michael handed Savannah the phone and she stepped back to take the picture. She laughed. "How cute is that?" She turned to Peter. "This shot could be the heart of your next big advertising campaign."

Once Savannah had taken a couple of photos and checked them over, Michael tugged on the leash again. But Rags continued to sit and stare. "Come on, big boy," he said.

He leaned over to pick up the cat when Rochelle said, "Wait. There may be something special about that painting."

Peter shook his head. "It's just a print. I have a lot of them. They're numbered. See, this one's number 312."

"What is significant about this piece? What inspired it?" she asked.

Peter thought about it for a moment and then answered, "I did that one when I first met Dawna. I actually had her in my mind while I was working on it. She kind of influenced that painting. For some reason it became popular, and I sell a lot of prints."

"Interesting," Rochelle said. "Now, does Rags sense her energy in this? Is he trying to tell us something?"

Peter rubbed his hand over his hair. "I doubt it," he said. "Her…*energy* is all over the place in here. She works here almost every day." He glanced down at the cat again and said, "Let's get out of here, shall we?"

Just as the two couples and the cat arrived home—this time taking the sidewalks instead of the beach—Peter's phone rang.

"What the…?" he mumbled. "Who's calling me this late? Hello," he said into the phone. "What? Damn. Okay, I'll be right there."

When Peter ended the call, he let out a deep sigh. "Michael, would you mind calling a cab for Rochelle?" he asked, handing him a twenty-dollar bill. "That was the police. They said my alarm at the shop is going off. Man, I don't know what's wrong. Must be a short in the system."

"Or someone saw us leave and broke in," Savannah suggested.

# Chapter 5

The next morning Savannah rolled out of bed just as Michael was coming from the bathroom wearing his board shorts.

"You're up early for someone who partied all night," she said, wrapping her arms around him.

He kissed her. "You, too. It was fun wasn't it?"

"Yes, it was quite an intense and interesting evening," she said. "Imagine us old fuddy-duddy parents having such a lovely adult evening out."

He buried his face in her neck and murmured, "Fuddy-duddy parents? I don't think so." He then stepped away from her, and slipped on a t-shirt. "I'm going to help Peter remove his paintings from the gallery this morning before it opens."

"Okay," she said, yawning. "See you later, then. Maybe Mom and I'll take Lily out to breakfast, if Mom hasn't already prepared a big meal for us."

"It's been great having her here, hasn't it? We've been waited on, and we're free to go out anytime we feel like it."

"Yes, like being back home with my parents. Mom's enjoying herself, too. She loves playing Grammy."

He walked over and kissed her again. "See you in a while. Let me know if you go out to eat; maybe I'll meet you there."

***

A couple of hours later, Michael joined Savannah and Gladys at Haps Cafe on the beach.

"So did you get all the paintings moved?" Savannah asked.

"Yeah, those that weren't damaged."

"What?"

"You know that call Peter got last night?"

Savannah nodded.

"Well, someone had thrown an open bucket of paint through the front window at the gallery and damaged all the art in that area. It affected a total of seven paintings."

"I heard about that," the server said, as he approached their table. "That's Peter Whitcomb's gallery, right? Some people were in here talking about it early this morning. Do they know who did it?"

Michael looked up at the server and shook his head. "What were they saying?" he asked.

"Oh, just that someone threw a paint bucket through the window." He hesitated and added, "They were kinda laughing about it like it was a joke or prank."

"Do you think these people had something to do with it?" Michael asked.

"Heck, I wondered that myself, the way they were talking."

"Do you know who they were?" Savannah asked.

The young man looked down and shook his head slowly. "Not really. I've seen them around the beach, though. They don't eat here often. One of them seems to come into some money every once in a while and he brings a few buddies in for breakfast. He was flashing a hundred-dollar bill this morning. I had trouble giving him change that early in the day."

Savannah was keenly interested now. "Uh, Tad," she said, reading from his name tag, "can you tell us what the people looked like?"

"Yeah, your typical homeless beach-bum type. The one with the money had brown hair and a beard. He wore a baseball cap with some sort of animal on it. I think it advertised a company with an animal's name."

"Like John Deere?" Michael asked.

"Yes, but it wasn't a deer, it was a smaller animal." He shook his head. "Gosh, I don't remember what it was. The hat was pretty dirty."

"Is there anything else you can remember about this guy?" Savannah asked.

Tad thought and then he said, "A tattoo. He had a stupid-looking face smoking a pipe tattooed on his hand."

"Smoking a pipe?" Michael asked.

"Yeah, with big cheeks and wearing a sailor's cap."

"Popeye," Savannah said.

Tad nodded. "Yeah, I guess." He looked around the café and said, "Hey, what can I get you folks to eat this morning?"

After they'd placed their order, Savannah leaned toward Michael and spoke quietly, "It sounds like someone paid that guy to damage Peter's paintings. But who?"

Michael took a sip of coffee. "Someone who's jealous, probably. Peter said nothing like this had ever happened to him before he started selling for the big dollars and exhibiting in the most prestigious shows."

"But not every artist has enemies," Gladys said, while feeding Lily pears from a jar with her baby spoon. "Why Peter?" she asked.

"Presumably because he's hanging around with the wrong people," Savannah said, as if deep in thought.

She looked across the table at Michael and glanced at her mother. Both of them stared back. She explained, "Well, Michael, isn't that pretty much what Rochelle said last night? And Blake said the same thing. He should be wary of the people closest to him, like Dawna, Kara, and…"

"Yes, I guess so," he said, "but Dawna showed up at the gallery before the glass company arrived to replace the window this morning, and she seemed genuinely upset by the scene there. She cried and tried to console Peter. I think she's the one who needed consoling. She was more upset than he was."

"What about Kara?"

"Didn't see her this morning."

"So did he open today?"

"Sure did," Michael said. "He had a large throw rug delivered and, after the cleaning service left, he put the new rug over the paint stains, replaced the damaged paintings with fresh prints, and opened the gallery."

"Did he tell Rochelle what happened?"

"Yes, he called her. Know what she said?"

Savannah grinned. "Well, she's too classy to say, 'I told you so.'"

"You got that right," Michael agreed. "No. She asked, 'what color?' Peter wasn't sure what she meant. When he questioned her, she said, 'What color paint was it?'"

"Really? I wonder why."

"She said she visualized red, and he told her it *was* red. Know what she said then?"

"No, what?" both women asked.

"'That's not a spiritual color.' She explained that red signifies power and physical need for earthly possessions, or something like that."

Savannah scoffed. "Well, it wasn't a spiritual action, that's for sure." She then asked, "How's Peter?"

"Oh, he's okay, I guess. Seems like he's been beaten down a little. But he perked up when he talked about Rochelle and last evening. I think he's smitten."

"As he should be," Savannah said. "She's genuine. I like her."

"And you don't like the other women he has brought around to meet us?"

"Well, Dawna's a little…difficult to read."

"You think so?" he asked.

"Yeah. She's nice enough, I guess, only there's something…not quite authentic about her. I'm not sure if it's her personality or whatever drives her, maybe. Something is not coming across to me as sincere."

Michael cringed a little. "Savannah, where do you get this stuff?"

"Listening to my inner voice, that's all, hon," she said, smiling demurely.

He shook his head. "Well, you've always had a pretty good sense about people and their motives…like your cat does." He looked at her for a moment, then said, "Maybe you should tell Peter about your impressions."

"Okay, I guess. But it's all rather vague in my mind—probably too ambiguous for him to embrace."

"Vannie, I never heard you talk like that before," Gladys scolded. "Have you been following some sort of cult?"

Savannah laughed. "No, it's probably my association with Iris. She's kind of metaphysical. It's rubbing off, I guess."

Gladys shook her head. "Well, it sounds foreign coming from you. You've always been my grounded, down-to-earth daughter. Brianna was more into the woo-woo stuff. Sure never thought I'd hear you talk like that. It's all blibber-blabber to me."

After breakfast, Michael asked, "What do you ladies have planned for today?"

"I thought I'd take Mom to see Peter's gallery," Savannah said.

Gladys smiled. "Oh, I'd like that. Is it far?"

Michael motioned with one hand. "Just down the street." He stretched in his chair and said, "I think I'll go on home and maybe take a nap." He winked. "I'm behind on my newspaper-reading, too."

"Okay, hon," Savannah said, standing and lifting Lily from the high chair. "We'll see you later, then."

"When are Iris and Craig coming?" he asked, before leaving.

"Sometime this afternoon—whenever Craig's meetings are over in Vegas."

"Good," he said. Once Savannah had Lily strapped into the stroller, Michael leaned in and kissed her. "'Bye." He waved before stepping away. "Have fun."

"Oh, I love that jewelry," Gladys said, stopping in front of a curio shop on their way to the gallery. "Let's go in and look at it. I want to pick up some little gifts for friends."

"Sure. Good idea. I want to get something for Auntie, too, since she and Max couldn't join us. Also Colbi and Damon, Helena…" She let out a sigh. "Yup, I guess I have some serious shopping to do."

***

Over an hour later, after browsing through several shops, Savannah and Gladys walked into Peter's gallery wheeling Lily in the stroller. "Hello," Dawna greeted cheerfully.

"Hi Dawna. This is my mother, Gladys Jordan. She wanted to see Peter's gallery."

"Hello," she said. "Welcome. Please look around

and let me know if you have any questions."

"I have one," Savannah said. "I saw a painting in here on my first visit. I think I want to buy it. I see it's not where it was. It's the one that looks like the Big Sur area."

"Oh yes," Dawna said. "I know the one you mean. It *is* Big Sur, actually. Let's see, I think it's in the first alcove. Come with me," she invited.

"Just look around, Mom," Savannah said. "I'll be right back."

"Is this it?" Dawna asked, pointing. "Let's see, it's called, *Point of Discovery.*"

"Oh, you gave me goose bumps," Savannah said. "That's pretty close to the spot where I made an important discovery in my life—I was at a crossroads." Savannah stared into the painting. After a few moments, she realized Dawna was speaking to her, and she turned to face her. "I'm sorry," she said. She blinked and shook her head a little. "Gosh, that painting really grabbed me and pulled me in."

Dawna laughed out loud. "I know how that can happen," she said.

Savannah gazed at the woman for a moment. *That's the first time I've seen her laugh. She's usually so uptight.* "So it isn't just me?" she asked, feeling a little embarrassed.

"No," Dawna said, putting her hand on Savannah's arm. "It doesn't happen often, but there are people who… well, who just relate to certain pieces of art." She looked melancholy for a moment and spoke almost under her breath. "Peter's art has that quality. I just wish I could attain it in my work."

"Oh, so are you painting again?" Savannah asked. "You said you used to paint."

Dawna looked up at Savannah, her eyes wide. She put her hand over her mouth. "Oh, no. Not really." When

Savannah looked confused, she said, "My contribution to the art world is through Peter—promoting his work. That's my passion."

Savannah peered at Dawna for a moment and then looked at the painting again. "How much is it?" she asked, quietly.

Dawna became contemplative. "It's one of his early works. I think he was still discovering himself. It was at the beginning of his transition to the style he has adopted. It's marked $300. These earlier works don't carry the prices the more recent ones do."

"Sold," Savannah said, smiling. "Can I pick it up later when we have the car out? It's a little large for us to manage after all the shopping Mom and I did this morning."

"Sure." Dawna said. She then asked, "What did you buy?"

"Gosh," Savannah said, waving her hand in the air in front of her, "jewelry, a little see-through box for my beach glass, a darling evening bag, a tote bag…Mom picked up a couple of gifts for friends. Oh, and I got an adorable replica of one of our cats—a little figurine."

Dawna continued to stare at Savannah. She looked at her watch and said, "Kara will be here in a few minutes. Would you like to have a mocha with me down at the coffee house? I'm ready for a break."

Savannah glanced at her watch. Just then they heard, "Vannie? Oh, there you are," Gladys said, as she spotted her daughter in the alcove.

"Mom, look at my painting. I just bought it," Savannah said, pointing to it.

"Oh, that's nice, honey," Gladys said. "I like beach scenes and ocean scenes. He does some beautiful work, doesn't he? I just bought some note cards from the other girl."

"Oh, is Kara here?" Dawna asked, walking out of the alcove and back to the main gallery. Savannah and Gladys followed.

"Vannie, the baby's getting tired. We should take her back to the house."

"Uh, okay, Mom. Dawna and I are going to have coffee, if you don't mind."

"No, not at all."

"Can you find it on your own?"

"Sure; all I have to do is stay on the street where all the houses face the ocean," she said, as she pushed the stroller toward the exit. Savannah followed Gladys and Lily out onto the sidewalk. "I have my cell if I need GPS help from Michael," Gladys said. "We'll be fine. You go drink your coffee."

Savannah knelt and kissed Lily's forehead. "Have a good nappy, sweetheart," she said. Lily rubbed one eye with her hand and then excitedly patted the stuffed chenille cat that sat in her stroller tray. Savannah stood and watched Gladys and the stroller disappear into a small crowd of people on the sidewalk and then she stepped back inside the gallery. She found a chair and sat while texting Michael that her mom was on her way back with Lily and that she would be along shortly, after having coffee with Dawna. When she looked up from her phone, she saw Kara appear from the back area.

"Hi Savannah. How are you today?" she asked.

"Great," she said. "Just waiting for Dawna."

"Oh, she's in the office. Go on back and let her know you're here."

"She knows I'm here. But, yeah, I'll let her know I'm ready," she said, taking long strides toward the back office. Suddenly, Savannah heard an angry voice. "You owe me, lady, and you'd better pay up or I'll go to the…"

"You'll get your money. Don't worry. Just get the hell out of here. I'll meet you this afternoon, like I said."

Savannah stopped in her tracks. *That's Dawna. Who's she talking to? Sounds like he's awfully angry. Gads, what should I do?* While Savannah tried to decide whether to walk in on the conversation or leave, Dawna emerged from the back room. They heard a door slam behind her. Dawna winced, but seemed to recover quickly when she saw Savannah. She took her by the arm and asked, "Are you ready?"

"Uh, yes," Savannah said. She glanced behind Dawna. "Is everything all right?"

"Oh sure. Just my landlord trying to collect the rent. He wants it on the twentieth no matter what. I just haven't been to the bank, that's all. No problem," she said, speaking faster than Savannah had heard her speak before.

Dawna led Savannah back into the main gallery. She pulled her purse out of a closet and said to Kara, "I'll be gone for a little while. Will you be okay until I get back?"

"Sure. Take your time."

Dawna turned to leave and then looked back at Kara as if she wanted to say something more. Instead, she continued through the door, Savannah following behind her. Once out on the street, Dawna scowled. "She's practically worthless around here. I don't know why Peter keeps her on." She glanced at Savannah, "Or maybe I do," she said, a look of disgust on her face.

"She seems pretty devoted to Peter's work," Savannah said.

Dawna looked at Savannah. "All an act," she said. "She's acting!" She motioned to the left. "Here, they have excellent designer coffee in here and some nice goodies. Peter and I get the baklava when they have it."

"Sounds good," Savannah said.

Once Dawna had received a baklava and her iced-blended mocha with whipped cream and Savannah had her chai, they found a table on a charming outside patio. Dawna remarked, "You can't see the ocean from here, but it has a nice atmosphere and it's quiet."

"It's lovely," Savannah said, glancing around at the array of large pots filled with flowering plants. "They can sure grow a lot of things along the coast down here that we can't grow."

"Whole different climate, isn't it?" Dawna said.

"Yes, and a whole different atmosphere," Savannah said. "It's so casual and fun here. I could get used to this life real fast." She looked at Dawna. "Have you always lived here?"

Dawna took a sip of her mocha and set the glass down. "No. I came here from New York City. I'm a Midwest native; moved to New York to start a career in art when I was in my early thirties. I managed a couple of galleries there over the years. Eventually I met Peter and, well, you know the rest of the story. I've been working with him for nearly seven years, now."

Savannah looked at her for a moment. "This is your career, isn't it, Dawna?"

The woman looked confused. "Huh?"

"You take this job very seriously—you seem to work awfully hard."

"Well, someone has to," she said, chuckling. "You've been keeping Peter busy." She studied Savannah and added, "He's gone a lot. So, yes, I have a lot of responsibility." She looked down at her coffee, stirring the whipped cream into it. "He pays me well, too. I have everything I could want in this job. Yes, it's my career."

"Then why…" Savannah started.

"What?" Dawna asked, frowning.

Savannah waved her hand, "Oh, never mind. None of my business."

"No, really. It's okay. Ask."

"Well, I was just wondering why you seem sad."

Dawna looked at Savannah. She took a deep breath and started to respond. Then she slumped a little and said, "You're quite astute, there." She stirred her coffee some more. "Yeah, I'm not totally happy. Not yet, anyway. Like most people, I had expectations that weren't met." She looked around the patio. "Maybe they never will be." She sat with her thoughts for a moment and then said, "Savannah, I…"

Savannah watched as Dawna tried desperately to hold back her emotions, but tears welled in her eyes. "I'm sorry," Savannah said, reaching across the table for her hand. "I didn't mean…"

Dawna shook her head. "Not your fault. I've just been so emotional lately. I'm the one who should apologize. It's just that…" she lowered her head and began to sob softly.

"What is it?" Savannah asked, quietly.

Dawna struggled to gain control. Finally, she said, "I don't know. Just pressure, I guess."

"Dawna," Savannah asked, "what is it that you're missing—that you need or want in your life? You aren't doing what so many women do and stuffing your own desires in order to pursue what you think is your path, are you? You don't seem to be that type of woman. You're accomplished; strong."

"Stuffing my desire to pursue my path…" Dawna repeated. "God, Savannah, is that what I'm doing?"

"I don't know, is it? Is there something else you would rather be doing with your life?" When Dawna didn't respond, Savannah leaned toward her and said, "Some of us take the wrong road and can't understand why it doesn't work. I had a friend in veterinary school who hated everything about veterinary science."

"But she went to school to become a veterinarian?"

"Yes, and she failed courses, struggled horribly with the classes, complained about the teachers. There was nothing about it that she enjoyed."

Dawna blotted at her eyes. "So why did she stay?"

"For a couple of reasons. One was because she had made the commitment. She couldn't stand the idea of admitting she may have been wrong in her decision. And she kept going because she expected to enjoy being a veterinarian. She loved animals, after all. It didn't occur to her that the very studies she disliked would become her life as a veterinarian."

"So what did she do? Did she become a vet, anyway?"

"She graduated, practically at the bottom of the class, but she never practiced. She happened to find her path quite by accident. Luckily, she opened up enough to recognize that it was her path. She met another woman who had recently started a nonprofit for pets left behind when their owners died or became too ill to care for them. She got involved. She's now the director of the organization and is happier than I've ever seen her. We communicate occasionally by email."

Dawna sighed. "But how does someone know it when they see it? I believe with my whole heart that this is where I should be, so why aren't I as happy as I should be?"

"I don't know. That's something you'll have to figure out within yourself." Savannah paused and then asked, "Do you meditate or reflect?"

Dawna laughed. "Not really. I'm pretty much all wound up most of the time." She held up her coffee drink. "This probably doesn't help."

"Ever try yoga?"

Dawna shook her head.

"Well, you have to be open in order to find your true path and you can't be open if your mind is always busy—always working. It helps me to make better decisions if I slow down a little. Take time out. You could walk on the beach late in the day or early in the morning when it's quiet. Shove all conscious thoughts—you know, of work, what to fix for dinner, and stuff like that—out of your mind. Free up your mind and see what comes to you naturally. I've been told that everything we need to know in order to make the best choices for ourselves is inside us somewhere. It's just a matter of being quiet long enough to release it and then trust it."

"Prayer," Dawna said.

Savannah smiled. "Bingo." She spoke more quietly, "…only rather than asking for something, we need to listen to what He wants us to know." Suddenly, Savannah frowned. "What's wrong, Dawna?" She turned to see what seemed to frighten the woman and saw an unkempt man staring in from outside the patio. Savannah's heart began to race. She asked, her voice strained, "Do you know him?"

Dawna shook her head, then looked down at her coffee. "Uh, no. I don't know him. He just looked a little scary, that's all. The homeless freak me out. You know, they think it was a homeless guy who broke in that night and stabbed me."

"Really?" Savannah said, lowering her brows. "I didn't hear that."

"Yes, I just wish they'd go to Duluth, or Chicago, or somewhere. I hate them," she said.

Savannah stared at her tablemate for a few moments and decided to change the subject. "Dawna do you have an outlet at all? You said you used to paint."

"Oh boy, did I," she said. "I painted nonstop for a few years after I met Peter." She spoke in a hushed voice. "I was a closet painter, you see."

Savannah noticed Dawna's demeanor shift. She relaxed a little. "You were happy then, weren't you?" she asked.

Dawna started to speak, but stopped. She tilted her head and looked at Savannah. "Yes, I was happy then." She spoke more slowly and quietly. "I have a lot of paintings in storage. Not too long ago, I spent nearly an entire day at my storage unit, just looking at all my work and dreaming of the day when I could paint seriously again. Yes, I miss my art terribly."

"Really?" Savannah said. "That's great. Creative endeavors do feed our soul, don't you think?"

"I'm beginning to believe that. Yes."

"So are you going to quit working for Peter and pursue your own art? Is that what you're thinking?"

Dawna pulled away from the table and looked at Savannah through eye slits.

"Hey," Savannah said, "it's just you and me here. I'm only prying because I'm interested," she laughed, "…and nosy."

Dawna smiled weakly and leaned closer to Savannah. "Well, I have the opportunity to start painting again. Recently, someone saw one of my pieces and offered me a partnership."

Savannah tilted her head. "Partnership? You mean you produce the art and he or she promotes it—like what you do for Peter?"

"Yeah, kinda."

"Well, I think that's wonderful. I'm sure Peter would be behind you one-hundred percent. If he's the kind of human being I think he is, he'll be happy to see you sprout your own wings of success."

"I guess," she said. "…only…"

"Only what?"

"I'm not sure I've handled the situation well. I think I've blown it." She dropped her head and began fidgeting with the remnants of her baklava, then looked at her watch. "I'd better get back to work," she said, as she picked up the bill and stood, lifting her purse and slinging it over one shoulder. Without looking at Savannah, she said, "Thanks for lending an ear. You gave me some things to think about. I just hope it's not too late for me."

"What are you talking about, Dawna? What are you, forty-something? A lot of artists get their big break late in life."

"Yeah, yeah, Monet, Van Gogh…I know. But I want it big and I want it now. I'm probably more ambitious than most." She looked at Savannah. "I will make it happen… one way or another," she said, turning and walking toward the bakery counter. "I'll be right back. Want to pick up a few things." Dawna returned carrying a pink box presumably filled with bakery treats. "Ready?" she asked, as she headed quickly out through the patio gate onto the sidewalk.

Savannah caught up with her and said, "I have no doubt that you can do it. I hope it all works out for you. But don't forget to breathe."

"Uh, oh, sure. I can do that. Thanks, Savannah."

"For what?" she asked.

"For listening. It means a lot. I don't have many friends. Don't have time." She looked at her watch again. "Gotta go. Let's chat later, shall we?"

Before Savannah could respond, Dawna was off like a shot, heading toward the gallery.

***

"Well, there you are," Michael said when Savannah walked out to the deck later that morning. "So how was your chat with Dawna…with a W?" he asked.

"Downright weird," she said, lowering herself into a deck chair and turning it to face him. "I'm still reeling from the experience."

Michael raised the back on his lounge chair. "What happened?"

Savannah was quiet for a moment then she tilted her head and asked, "Have you ever seen someone's face change right before your eyes?"

"What?" he said. "Do you mean like when Lily is crying and I tickle her and she starts laughing?"

Savannah shook her head. "No. I mean like from… well, pretty to grotesque."

"What? Where have you been—to a wax museum with a hot blow dryer?"

Savannah laughed. "No."

"To see a rubber man at the circus?"

"No, Michael. You're being silly."

"Well, what do you mean, then? Did you see some woman's facelift fall?"

"No, it's Dawna."

"Dawna? What happened, did she burn herself lighting a cigar?"

"Michael, stop it and let me tell you," she insisted. "I was listening to her talk about something. She looked… you know…attractive. She's basically an attractive woman. She has nice eyes, her brows have a good arch, her skin is pretty."

"Was she smiling?" he asked.

"Not exactly. She was just telling me a story. But as she talked, her face changed. Her eyes grew kinda dark and lifeless, her skin tone was dull. It was as if her whole facial structure changed and she became someone else right there in front of me."

Michael frowned. "Do you mean visually? She actually looked that different to you?"

Savannah nodded. "Yes!" she exclaimed.

"Had the lighting changed or something?" he asked.

No," she said. "It's just that the more she talked about her life and how basically unhappy and unfulfilled she is, the more unattractive she became. Her features changed. I'm not kidding, Michael. Her features changed right before my eyes." She paused; looked down at her hands. "It was not a pretty picture." When Savannah finished speaking, she noticed that Michael was quiet, as if he were trying to digest what she'd just told him. "Ever have something like that happen before?" she asked.

"No," he said, shaking his head. "Can't say as I have. Good lord, it must have been a weird experience. I can't imagine."

"I'll bet Iris could imagine. I can't wait to talk to her about this." She looked at her watch. "They could be coming in just about any time."

***

"Aunt RisRis! Uncle Craig!" Savannah shouted when the couple appeared with Michael on the deck later that day. "I'm so happy to see you two."

"Long drive, but worth it," Iris said. "This is gorgeous. Can't wait to get out of my clothes and into the sun."

"This isn't a nudey beach, babe," Craig said.

"I know; I have my suit."

"Well, come on, we'll show you to your room and you can change." Savannah slipped into her light-weight cover-up and then hugged both Iris and Craig. "Do you want a beautiful room with a mountain view or a plain room with an ocean view?" she asked.

The couple looked at each other.

"Show them both," Michael suggested, "then they can decide."

"Okay, come on, girlfriend," Savannah said, looping one arm through Iris's and leading the couple toward the staircase. "Here's the beautiful room," she said as they stepped into the first room at the top of the stairs.

Iris twirled around slowly and spoke almost reverently. "Oh, this is so nice. I love it." She looked at Savannah. "…but let us see the ocean view room."

When they walked into the room downstairs and Iris saw the large windows leading to a deck overlooking the beach, she swooned. "Oh yes. Let's take this one. I love this one, don't you, Craig?"

"Sure, whatever you want."

"You could sleep in one tonight and the other the next night," Michael suggested when he caught up with the trio.

"Sure could," Iris said, considering the idea. She then said, "Naw, I want to hear the ocean all night long. Yes, this is the one."

"Let's bring your things in, then," Michael said, heading out through the door.

"We'll meet you on the deck in a few," Savannah said, turning to leave.

"Can I get you an iced tea or lemonade?" Savannah offered when the couple returned to the deck in their beach attire. Iris wore a large floppy pink hat over her red hair, a matching pink floral one-piece swimsuit with a lace cover-up, and pink flip-flops with a plastic flower across her perfectly manicured toes.

"Well, I guess you *have* worn board shorts before, Craig," Michael said. "You've got a bit of a tan going on there."

"Yeah, we've been to the mountain cabin a few times lately, and I worked around the place without my shirt. Got a little color," he said, examining his arms and legs.

"You still need your sunscreen," Iris said. She then asked Savannah, "Where's the sweet baby patooty? Napping?"

"Yes, she and Mom usually nap this time of day, if we aren't dragging them to Disneyland or someplace."

"Oh, did you take her to Disneyland? How did she like it?"

"Yes, and Adam, too. I'll show you my pictures in a minute. We all had such a good time."

Once they had settled on the deck with beverages and an assortment of veggies, fruit, and dip, Craig asked, "So you've been having fun, huh?"

"Yes," Savannah said, "except…"

"There's your cat!" Iris exclaimed. "Oh my God, you brought him with you?"

"Sure did," Michael said, laughing. "And the dog, Buffy, and Walter. Everyone's here."

"That's just plain crazy," Iris said. "Who travels with their cats?"

"Veterinarians, that's who," Craig said. "I travel with my gun."

Both Michael and Savannah looked at him. "You do?" she said.

"Well, yeah."

Iris jumped into the conversation. "There must have been hundreds of guns at the conference Craig attended in Vegas. Law-enforcement people carry guns on and off duty."

Savannah shivered a little. "Oh. I never thought about it. So there's a gun in this house?"

"I can leave it in the car if it bothers you," Craig offered.

"Rags wants out," Iris said. "Do you let him out?"

"Yeah, he's been out," Michael said. "Sometimes because we let him out and sometimes not."

"He saved a life last week," Savannah said.

Iris raised her sunglasses. "What?"

Craig chuckled. "Did he pull someone from a riptide?"

"No," Savannah said. "He brought home a bloody necklace and we found out who it belonged to. She had been stabbed and we called an ambulance."

Michael chuckled. "He also stole a gal's bathing-suit top."

Craig's eyes lit up. "Now that, I'd like to see."

Iris quickly put her hand protectively against her chest. "Well, he'd better not try that with me."

Everyone laughed.

"Oh," Savannah said, putting her hand on Iris's arm, "he has a reputation."

Iris scoffed. "Well, yeah."

"But I mean, it's wider than we thought. The gal whose top he took—well—she had read about Rags on the Internet."

"Really?" Iris said, glancing at the cat, who continued to peer out through the sliding glass doors.

"Tell us more about the gal who got stabbed," Craig said.

"Oh, she's Peter's gallery manager," Savannah started.

"Peter's the owner of this house," Michael explained. "He's an old friend of mine from college and he's an artist with a gallery along the beach. I'm sure you'll get a chance to meet him."

"So someone broke in and attacked her?" Craig asked.

"We think so. It's all rather vague. In fact, she's kind of hard to read. Iris, I actually wanted to talk to you about her."

"Me? Why?"

"I thought maybe you could give us a perspective. I guess you'd have to meet her first, but I can tell you, she's a puzzle."

"Oh, look who's up from her nap," Iris said, smiling, when Gladys appeared on the deck with Lily in her arms. "Hello, Mrs. Jordan," Iris said, approaching her. "Hi, Miss Lily. How's the little mermaid? You look so cute in your sundress." She looked at Gladys. "Can I hold her?"

"Yes. She's ready for a bottle; want to give it to her?"

"Sure do," Iris said. "Come to Aunt RisRis, little angel," she cooed. "Can we take her down to the beach after she eats?" she asked.

Savannah nodded. "Yeah, we can do that."

"But she can't go in the water," Michael said, sternly.

"Why?" Craig asked. "Waves too big?"

"Well, that, too, I guess," Michael responded. "But she got stung by a jellyfish a few days ago. Don't want a repeat visit to the ER."

"Oh, poor baby," Iris said, cuddling her close.

Craig encouraged Lily to grip his finger with her little hand. "A jellyfish? That's not good." He looked at Michael. "She's okay?"

"Oh yes, but Savannah and I are still recovering from the ordeal."

***

"So did you have a powwow with Iris yesterday?" Michael asked Savannah as they prepared to go down for breakfast the next day.

"Yes," Savannah said, taking a t-shirt out of the closet and pulling it on over her bathing- suit top. She lifted her wet hair off her neck and said, "Rochelle joined us."

"Really?" Michael asked. "When?"

"When you and Craig took Lily down to get those groceries, Iris and I were walking on the beach and ran into Rochelle. She lives across town, but drives down here to walk on the beach when she can." Savannah entered the bathroom and began blow-drying her blond hair.

Michael followed her. "So did you bring up Dawna's odd behavior—that face-change thing?" he asked, while lathering up to shave.

"What?" she asked, shutting off the dryer.

"Did you talk about Dawna?"

"Yeah. Let me dry my hair a little and I'll tell you about it." She started to turn the dryer back on, but stopped and said, "Hey Michael, go get us some coffee and let's enjoy it on our lanai, shall we?"

He frowned. "Lanai?"

"Yes, that's what they call a small balcony in Hawaii."

"You're not in Hawaii, Savannah."

She winked. "I can be if I want to be."

"Let me shave first, okay?"

She looked at him and said, "Why don't you leave some stubble? We're on vacation and I think you're sexy with that unshaven look."

Michael thought about his wife's comments for a few seconds. "Sexy, huh?" He caught Savannah's eye in the mirror, grinned his sideways grin and began wiping the shaving cream off his face. "Be back in a hot minute," he said, as he dashed out the bathroom door. When he returned carrying two cups of coffee and two blueberry muffins on a small tray, he found Savannah sitting on the balcony staring out over the ocean. "Your daughter says 'good morning.'"

"What's she doing?" Savannah asked, smiling.

"Well," he cleared his throat, "when I left, she was wiping strained peaches on Rags's tail."

"What?"

"Your mom was feeding her and she put her hand in the bowl. Before Gladys could wipe it off, Rags walked by and Lily grabbed his tail," he said, chuckling.

"Well, he probably loved licking the cereal and peaches off. He likes fruit, you know. I used to share my morning fruit with him when he was a kitten."

"Yeah, he was licking his tail vigorously when I left."

"Ahhh, this is the life," isn't it, Michael?" Savannah said. "Look how the water sparkles this morning. Ever notice how the water changes color and texture? The view is ever-changing. I just love it here, don't you?"

"Yes. It's been great. But we have a pretty nice life in Hammond, don't you think?"

"Sure. I love our life, our home, our friends. But I've really enjoyed this respite—this totally different way of living." She thought for a moment. "I guess this is how the rich and famous live—they play all the time, and they probably don't appreciate it nearly as much as we do."

"You don't think so?" he asked.

"Well, no, because it's their lifestyle. It's what they do. It's special to us, but probably not so much to those who live this way all the time."

Michael took a bite of his muffin. After washing it down with a swig of coffee, he said, "So, tell me about your visit with Rochelle and Iris."

Savannah set her coffee cup down. "Oh yes. Very interesting, actually. Rochelle said she met Dawna when she stopped at the gallery one night to pick up Peter for an early dinner. She said she's concerned about her."

"Does she think Dawna's in danger?"

"Yes, although probably not from outside herself—but inside."

"Huh?"

"She's a danger to herself, Michael. At least that's what Rochelle picked up from meeting her. When I told her and Iris some of my impressions, Iris said that Dawna may have some deep issues that are close to the surface. She could be close to losing it—as in having a nervous breakdown or something."

"Wow, like a time-bomb? Will she implode?"

"Well, Rochelle says you don't want to be in the way when someone boils over; you just don't know what they'll do."

"So why is she in this state?" Michael asked.

"Who knows?" Savannah said. "Rochelle says it's probably tied to a deep-seated anger stemming from disappointment or jealousy, maybe." She took a sip of coffee before saying, "Jealousy could stem from disappointment, I guess."

"Did you tell them about Dawna's face changing?" he asked in an almost mocking way.

She sat quietly for a moment and then said, "Actually, I did. Iris had experienced something similar once and she told us about it. We were both interested in Rochelle's input. Iris said she was so freaked-out when it happened to her that she never told anyone about it until now."

"So what did Rochelle say?" Michael asked.

Savannah took a breath. "Well, she said she doesn't know for sure, but her instinct is that when this happens, we're actually seeing that person's inner core—it's a peek into their true self—the self that's motivating their actions, their negative emotions." She shifted in her chair. "Michael, you know how sometimes you meet someone who you don't think is particularly good-looking…but the more you get to know that person, they actually become prettier—there's a sort of more pleasing quality to their appearance? Have you had that happen?"

"Um, well, I guess." After thinking about it for a moment, Michael said, "I used to think Iris's son, Damon was an unattractive guy—but that's when he was doing drugs. Now that he's all cleaned up and contributing to society, he's really a nice-looking man. Is that what you mean?"

"Kind of, yes. But with Damon, his transformation was because of a healthier lifestyle…and a healthier state of mind. What we discussed yesterday was something a bit more mysterious, I guess. But yeah, Rochelle told Iris and me that what we experienced was of a…higher power. We had a glimpse into another level of the person's personality or psyche." She took a sip of coffee. "I guess we all have good and bad elements inside us. Most normal people try to behave in public, so you see the person they want others to see. Someone who harbors a lot of hatred, anger, jealousy, for example—may display that negativity all the time or sometimes. And it can actually be visible in their facial features." She paused for a moment. "We don't question it when we see someone who is down on his luck, or living a horrible life. We expect to see the anger in his demeanor and even his features. But it's not expected when the individual is attempting to live a split life—successful on the outside and miserable on the inside."

Savannah took a sip of coffee. "I asked Iris about the friend she had this experience with—if she or he ever demonstrated negative tendencies."

"And what did she say?" Michael asked, obviously interested now.

"She said it was someone she dated for a while. When she saw the transformation, it scared her a little, but she didn't take it all that seriously. Guess what?"

"What?" he asked.

"A few months later, the dude went down for murder. It seems he was living a respectable life only on the outside. Under it all, he was a conniving crook. According to Rochelle, when something evil starts eating at you, it begins to surface in unique ways."

"Hey, was that…?" he started.

"The guy Rags identified as a murderer a few years ago?"

"Yes!"

"I'm pretty sure it was," Savannah said.

"Vannie," Gladys said, from behind them.

"Oh hi, Mom. Come on out and enjoy our balcony with us," Savannah said.

"Yeah, our lanai," Michael said, gesturing flamboyantly. He offered Gladys his chair. He then pulled a chair from the room out onto the small balcony, took Lily from Gladys, and sat down with her. "Did you finish feeding yourself and all the animals?" he asked the baby.

"Oh, this was a messy morning," Gladys said. "She had the cereal and peaches all over the place. She's one determined young lady, that one."

"Determined?" Savannah asked.

"Yes, she knows her mind and is starting to express it," she explained.

"Oh no," Michael lamented.

"What?" Savannah asked, frowning.

"Two women making demands…I don't know if I can stand it," he said.

Gladys laughed. She patted his shoulder. "Get used to it, Michael. With three females in the house, Vannie's father quickly learned to just say, 'Yes.'"

"Oh, is that how it goes?" he asked, shaking his head. "Well, both of my girls have me wrapped around their little fingers already. And do you know what?"

"What?" Gladys asked, looking at him skeptically.

He glanced at Savannah and said, "It's just where I want to be."

Gladys smiled. "You're a good man, Michael."

***

"Hi Peter, come meet some friends of ours," Michael said when the artist joined them on the deck later that afternoon. "Iris and Craig Sledge, this is Peter Whitcomb."

"Hey, you're the one who painted that picture in our bedroom," Iris said, excitedly.

Peter smiled. "Probably. Which one is it?"

"It's labeled *Dancing in the Light*. It's…well, just stunning," she said, practically swooning.

"Yeah," Craig said. "She stood there and stared at it for hours, talking about the light and the dark of it."

"Oh Craig," Iris scolded. Then she said to Peter, "It's just so interesting. I could look at it for hours."

"Better than your ocean view?" Michael asked.

"Just about," she said.

"I have prints of that painting at the gallery, if you're interested. I'll give you my family discount."

"We'll be down. Thank you," she said.

"What's that you have there? Treats?" Savannah asked.

He nodded. "Want one?" He opened the box he held to reveal a variety of bakery items—cookies, two red-velvet cupcakes, a few chocolate mini-cupcakes, and one piece of baklava.

"Sure," Savannah said, taking the box from Peter. "Let me put these on a platter. I just made some coffee."

"Before you go," Peter said, grabbing the baklava, "this one's mine." When Savannah feigned a scowl, Peter said, "Hey, I'm celebrating."

"Oh, what are you celebrating?" Michael asked.

"It was touch-and-go there for a while, but my work was selected to hang in a home that's being used in a new TV smash hit. It's something we've been working on for months and we've been side-lined by a lot of snags." He walked to a chair in the shade and sat down. "I don't know what happened. There seemed to be a disconnect in our communication with the jury and we almost lost the opportunity."

"Well, congratulations," Michael said.

"Yes, that's way cool," Savannah said, before walking away with the box of pastries.

Iris followed her into the kitchen. When they returned, the women set a tray of freshly poured coffee and a platter of the pastries on the table and everyone moved their chairs around it.

"Yum, red-velvet," Craig said, taking a cupcake and placing it on a small plate in front of him. He looked at Peter. "This isn't your favorite, too, is it?"

Peter smiled and shook his head.

"I'll have cookies," Michael said. "…good for dunking."

Peter took a small bite of the baklava, then set it on his plate. He picked up the coffee mug and cupped it in his hands. "Another nice day, huh?"

Michael nodded and dipped his second cookie into his coffee.

"Is it always this nice?" Craig asked.

"Oh no. We get what they call the marine layer. It loves to hug the beaches, especially this time of year. We haven't had much this year. So we picked a good one for you to visit." He turned to Savannah. "Are you enjoying yourself?"

"Oh gosh, yes," she said with emotion. "It's been wonderful. We can't thank you enough for…"

Peter put his hand up. "I'm glad you're here. You've been…well, your support means a lot." Just then he reached into his jeans pocket and pulled out his phone. He looked at the screen, pressed his lips together, and stood, walking away to take the call. "Gotta go guys," he said, after ending the call. "They need me at the gallery." He started to leave and then picked up his plate and cup and headed for the kitchen.

"Hey, don't bother with that. I'll get it," Savannah said.

He winked. "Heck no, you're on vacation." When he returned, he said, "See y'all later," before bounding down the deck steps and heading up the beach.

"Well, that was a short visit," Savannah said.

Michael grinned. "Yeah, like he said, *he's* not on vacation."

Iris turned to her husband. "Hey Craig, let's take a walk on the beach. I want to look for shells."

"Sure," he said. He turned to Savannah and Michael. "Want to go?"

The two of them looked at each other and both shook their heads. Michael responded, "Naw, I think I'll sit that one out."

"Lily should be up soon and I want to spend some time with her," Savannah said.

The couple had just left the deck when Gladys appeared. "Look who's up from her nap."

Savannah reached out and took the baby. "Oh, you're wearing your little bathing-suit. Wanna go swimming?"

"Swimming?" Gladys asked.

Savannah smiled. "I filled her plastic pool and left it out so the sun would warm the water." She lifted the piece of plastic she'd laid over the top and felt the water. "Nice and warm." She slipped off her shorts, took the baby from Gladys, and climbed into the pool with her.

"Oh, look at that—she is a little pollywog, isn't she?" Gladys said, snapping pictures of the baby with her phone.

"Hand me those toys, would you, Michael?" Savannah asked.

"Aww, a rubber ducky. Now isn't that cute?" Gladys said, snapping more pictures of the baby surrounded by her pool toys.

"That *is* cute," Savannah agreed. "Hey, Michael, get some pictures to send to everyone back home."

"Look at Daddy, baby girl," he said, trying to get her attention.

After a while, Savannah said, "Michael, would you get a dry towel for Lily? I think she's had enough swimming." She watched as he stepped into the house, but he didn't come back right away. "What's he doing in there?" she asked out loud, not expecting an answer.

Gladys, who was on a lounge chair watching Lily and Savannah in the little pool, craned her neck to peer through the windows. "It looks like he's in the kitchen doing something," she said.

Suddenly, Michael stepped outside through the sliding doors and announced, "Lexie's sick. I think she ate something. She's throwing up."

"Oh no," Savannah said, climbing out of the pool with Lily. She grabbed her terry cover-up, handed it to her mother, and said, "Here, Mom, use this to dry her off." She then reached for a slightly damp beach towel, wrapped it around herself and ran toward the house. "What happened, Michael?" Savannah asked as she walked into the kitchen and saw him kneeling on the floor comforting Lexie. Rags sat on the table watching.

"I don't know. I think maybe she was trying to eat that piece of baklava, because she vomited it up almost whole. It appears that she also tried to swallow some sort of plastic thing and I think that's what caused her to vomit."

Savannah lowered her brows. "Well, that's odd. I've never known her to eat a foreign object, have you?"

"No," he said, as he continued to gently rub Lexie's head.

Just then, Rags jumped down from the table and walked over to where Lexie lay. He bumped up against

Michael with his head and then rubbed against him before ambling toward the open wastebasket.

At the same time, Savannah peered into the wastebasket. "What plastic thing?" she asked.

"It's right there on the top with the baklava. Maybe under the napkin I used to pick it up. It's a pink doodad."

Savannah picked up the baklava with the napkin and turned it over to examine it. When she did so, it fell apart and a large piece dropped to the floor. "Oh, I see it," she said, straining to get a closer look.

Just then she heard a voice calling, "Hello…"

Savannah turned and was surprised to see Blake at the sliding door. "Hi," she said. "Come on in."

The PI stepped inside. "Thanks." She looked from Savannah to Michael and Lexie. "Everything okay?" she asked.

"I think so," Michael said. "Lexie just got into the trash and it appears that she was punished for it."

"Yeah, karma," Savannah said, grinning.

"What happened?" she asked, a look of concern on her face.

Just then Rags walked up to the piece of baklava Savannah had dropped and began examining it. Before she could stop the cat, he sniffed it briefly and then viciously attacked it with one violent swat of his paw.

"Wow!" Blake said. "If that wasn't aggressive!"

Savannah sighed. "Yeah it was." She turned toward Michael and asked quietly, "Did you see that?"

He nodded, solemnly. He then took a deep breath and asked Blake, "Do you happen to have access to a lab where we could have this analyzed?"

"What? Why?" she asked, frowning.

"Well, Rags has this uncanny ability to communicate strong messages like what you just saw. Savannah, would you agree that there could be something wrong with the baklava?"

She nodded. "That's what I was thinking."

They both looked at Blake, expectantly.

"Well, yeah, I actually do have a connection at a lab…" she started to say, when Savannah interrupted.

"Oh my gosh," she almost shouted, "Peter ate some of it!"

"It may be nothing," Michael said, in an attempt to keep things calm. "Anyway, he couldn't have eaten much. There's quite a bit here."

Blake peered at the couple for a moment, then pulled out her phone. "I'll make a call. Put it in something clean—preferably paper, not plastic," she instructed.

After a few minutes, Blake pushed her phone into the pocket of her Capris and reported, "He said to bring it on down. I'm on foot. Want to drive me over there, Savannah? It's just five miles or so from here."

"Sure, let me get some clothes on."

***

Forty-five minutes later, Savannah called Michael's cell phone. "It's contaminated," she said, choking back emotion. It probably would have killed Lexie if she'd kept it down. We're going to stop by the gallery before coming home. How is she?"

"She's fine," he said. "She's right here with us on the deck under the umbrella." He chuckled. "All she needs is a pair of shades."

"Shades?" Savannah asked.

"Sunglasses."

"Oh," she said. "I get it. See you later, Michael."

"Gads, parking is kind of a problem around here, isn't it?" Savannah said, as she drove slowly along the narrow streets searching for a parking place near the gallery.

Blake laughed quietly. "Yes, we should have taken the car back to the beach house and walked down."

"Here's a spot," Savannah said, as she pulled in. She laughed. "But you're right. We'll be walking farther than we would have if we'd gone home."

"Oh well, Savannah, I'm sure you didn't get that great figure looking for the closest parking space," Blake observed.

Savannah chuckled.

Within a few minutes, the two women stepped into the gallery. "Hi Savannah," Dawna said. She then noticed Blake and her demeanor became noticeably more rigid. "Oh, hello," she greeted without enthusiasm.

"Is Peter here?" Blake asked.

"Uh…he's…" she started.

Just then the gallery door opened and Peter stepped in. "Savannah, Blake…" he said. "Two of my favorite people. What are you doing down here…" He glanced from one to the other, a puzzled look on his face, "…together?"

"Can we talk to you, Peter?" Blake asked.

"Sure," he said, leading the two women toward his office.

"Uh, maybe we should go…somewhere," Blake suggested.

Peter looked confused. "Is everything all right?"

Blake glanced at Dawna again and said, "Sure. Just need to talk. Come on, I'll buy you a cup of coffee."

"No," Peter protested. "No more coffee. I've had way too much coffee today. Please, spare me." His demeanor perked up. "How about a beer?"

"Sure, a beer. Whatever you want," Blake said.

"Okay if I have Michael and our friends come down?" Savannah asked Blake quietly as they walked together away from the gallery.

"Yeah," she said. "Tell them we'll be at The Hut, a half block south of the gallery."

By the time Savannah, Blake, and Peter had placed their drink orders, Michael arrived with the Sledges. He introduced them to Blake and the server took their orders. "Cool joint," Craig said, looking around.

Peter nodded. "Yeah, it's a fun place." He then turned to Savannah and Blake and asked, "Okay, now why did you two kidnap me?"

"Peter," Blake said, "we think someone may have tried to poison you."

"What?!" he almost shouted. He looked around to make sure his outburst went unnoticed, leaned in toward his PI, and asked, "What are you talking about?"

"That baklava you were eating was contaminated with some sort of poison." She motioned toward Michael and Savannah and said, "Their dog tried to eat some out of the trash and got sick."

"Well, I think she vomited because she got a piece of plastic caught in her throat," Michael corrected.

Savannah nodded. "And Rags let us know there was something wrong with the baklava Lexie had vomited up, then Blake and I took it to have it tested."

Peter looked from one to the other of his tablemates, sat back in his chair and, with a confused look on his face, he said, "What?"

"Maybe I can explain," Michael said.

"No, I think I get it—the dog tried to eat it, threw it up, the cat…" he drew his eyebrows together. "…what exactly did the cat do?"

"Well, he swatted really aggressively at it."

When Peter gave him a blank look, Craig started to chuckle. "You gotta listen to that cat. He knows a piece of evidence when he sees it. He's helped me solve a lot of cases with his keen sense of…" he shrugged. "I don't know what it is, but he knows when there's something wrong."

Savannah nodded. She then said, "Anyway, Blake has a friend at a lab and we asked him to analyze it."

"Yes," Blake said, "and it was tainted, all right." She leaned forward. "Peter, where did you get the baklava?"

"Oh my gosh," Savannah said. She grabbed Michael's arm. "All of us ate stuff out of that bakery box."

Blake's eyes pierced Savannah's. "You didn't tell me that."

"It just occurred to me," she said. "There was only one piece of baklava in there and all these other goodies."

"Is there anything left?" Blake asked, looking from the Iveys to the Sledges.

"Maybe a few cookies and a cupcake," Savannah said.

"We can have the other things analyzed, but if you're all feeling okay, I'm sure they weren't touched."

"Yeah, I'm fine—how about you, hon?" Savannah asked Michael. She looked at Craig and Iris. "And you guys?"

Craig grabbed his throat and began to make choking sounds. He then smiled and said, "I'm okay."

"I feel great," Michael said. He then frowned. "What

about you, Peter?"

"I'm okay. I took a small bite of the baklava before I got that phone call. It tasted a little funny. I decided I wasn't in the mood for it and tossed it."

"Where did you get the pastries?" Blake asked.

Peter answered promptly. "At the office. We take turns bringing things in to share. Everyone knows baklava is my favorite."

"Who brings these things in?" Blake persisted.

"I do, Kara does, a couple of our neighboring gallery and shop owners stop in with goodies sometimes. Occasionally, a customer will bring something by. Just this week, while I was gone, Dawna said our customers Gerald and Tina brought in some homemade cookies."

"Does Dawna contribute?"

"Oh yes," Peter said, "Dawna picks up treats once in a while."

"So who brought that box in that you took to the Iveys today?" Blake asked.

"Uh, I'm not sure. I'll have to ask."

"It was probably Dawna," Savannah said. "I had coffee with her this morning and she bought a box of pastries."

# Chapter 6

That evening after a light dinner, Savannah, Michael, and Gladys entertained their guests on the deck. The five of them were wrapped in blankets next to the fire pit, sipping wine, and discussing the type of creatures they'd seen in the tide pools that afternoon, when Michael received a text.
*Rochelle and I are just getting home from an early dinner. Got wine?*

Michael made eye contact momentarily with each of the others. "Want to share the rest of our evening with Peter and Rochelle?" he asked.

Savannah yawned and said, "Why not? I'm on vacation."

Within a few minutes, the couple appeared, coming up the steps onto the deck. "Hi," Peter called. "Enjoying the cool evening?"

"Yes, it did turn a bit chilly tonight," Savannah said. "This is the first time since we've been here that I've worn a pair of jeans and a sweatshirt. All we need is a rainstorm and I'll feel right at home," she said, laughing. She looked at Peter and Rochelle. "Hey, do you want blankets?"

"No, I'm fine," Peter said, settling into a deck chair. "…but I will have a glass of that wine. What about you, Rochelle?"

Gladys stood up from her chair. "Here, take mine. I think I'll join Lillianna in slumber. Being at the beach wears me out."

Rochelle said, "Thanks." She took the blanket and laid it over the chair Gladys had vacated and then asked Savannah, "Can I help you?"

"Sure, come on," Savannah invited.

When the women returned with two glasses of wine and a new bottle, they heard Michael ask Peter, "Where'd you go for dinner?"

"An Italian place across town. They have great lasagna, just like Mama Maria makes."

Savannah tilted her head. "I thought Mama Maria was Mexican. She's Italian?"

"No, but she can cook like she is."

"By the way," Savannah said, "the other pastries tested clean."

"Good," Peter said. "I figured so, since no one got sick—only the poor dog. Is she okay?"

"What happened?" Rochelle asked, looking from one to the other.

"Oh, I almost ate a spoiled baklava. The dog found it and got sick. Blake had it analyzed and it appears that someone messed with it—someone wanted to hurt me," he said, thinning his lips.

"Oh," she said, frowning. "I was afraid of that. But I thought I'd dispensed enough protective light to squelch it."

"Apparently you did," Savannah said, grinning. "Everyone's just fine."

She smiled and looked at Peter. "Well, that's true. Just be careful, Peter, will you?" she said, leaning close to him. She cocked her head and asked, "Did they ever determine what happened that night you found your gallery manager—what's her name—Dawna, injured and bleeding?"

"What do you mean?" he asked. "Someone broke in through an open window and stabbed her."

Rochelle looked at Savannah and sighed before saying, "I think she did this to herself."

Peter looked shocked. "What?" he asked.

"She has issues, Peter," Rochelle explained.

"Nothing was missing, right?"

Michael broke in, "…except the jewelry Rags took."

"Wounds were shallow."

"But she bled a lot. She almost died," Peter insisted.

"Yes, because she hit a fairly large vessel," Rochelle said. "She's depressed, can't you see that?"

Peter thought about her comment before saying, "Unhappy, kinda confused, stressed-out, she may have a personality disorder of some sort, but I don't think she'd do something as bizarre as that to herself." He fidgeted with the zipper on his jacket. "Can we change the topic?"

"Sure," Rochelle said. "What would you like to talk about?"

"Um…how about you?" he said, smiling.

"Yes, I'm interested in knowing more about you," Savannah said.

"Me, too," Iris said.

Rochelle smiled. "I have few secrets."

"Yeah, that's what I want to know about—the secrets," Peter said, grinning. "And I want to know if you can foresee any more damage at the gallery, or any danger. Is all that stuff over?"

She shook her head. "Sadly, I see bull's-eyes all over you, Peter. No. I'm sorry, but you are not out of the crosshairs, yet."

Savannah and Iris exchanged glances.

After a little while, Peter sat upright and asked, "Hey, is everyone ready to go?"

"Go where?" Savannah asked.

He squirmed in his seat. "Didn't I tell you about the art walk tonight? It's a tour of the galleries. Everyone brings their wares out onto the sidewalk, there's music. It's rather festive. I don't know about you guys, but I'd like to be in a festive atmosphere."

Savannah and Michael looked at each other and then at the others.

Iris sat up straight. "Sounds like fun to me," she said. "Want to go, Craig?"

He groaned and frowned. "And leave all this comfort?"

"Come on, you party-pooper. Let's get out and have some fun."

Craig looked at Michael. "Are you going?"

Michael glanced at Savannah. "I'm pretty sure I am."

"Then I guess I'd better, too," Craig said.

Savannah stood. "Great! Let's go freshen up. I can be ready in ten minutes…what about you, Iris?"

Craig looked at Iris and laughed out loud. "Well, we'll catch up with you guys sometime tomorrow morning, if I know my wife."

"Oh Craig, stop," Iris said, heading for the sliding doors into the house. "I'll get my walking shoes and mad money and I'll be right out." She looked back at Craig, who appeared stunned. "Well, come on, old man," she said. "Whatsa matter, can't keep up?"

***

"This *is* festive," Iris said. "Look at all the twinkling lights everywhere and the art along the sidewalk. Makes me want to buy something."

"Well that's the idea," Peter said, smiling.

"I knew I should have left my wallet home," Craig complained.

"Hey, isn't that Kara?" Savannah said, pointing.

"Where?" Peter and Michael asked. Then Peter said, "Oh, I see. Looks like Charlynn with her." He laughed. "Those two are like conjoined twins. They're always together." He squinted a little. "Who's that they're talking to?" he wondered out loud.

"Looks like…" Savannah started. Oh my gosh, Peter, that's the man who keeps scaring me!"

"Scaring you?" Rochelle asked.

"Yes, I saw him looking at me through the window in Peter's office. Then I saw Dawna arguing with him." She turned to Peter. "He scared Dawna the other day when we were having coffee."

"What was he doing?" he asked.

"Staring at her through the vines on the patio at the coffee house."

As the group drew closer to Peter's gallery, they noticed that a transaction was taking place. "Did I just see Charlynn hand that guy an armload of paintings?" Peter asked. "What is she doing?" he hastened his pace. By the time he'd made his way through the sidewalk-clogging crowd, the man was gone. "What's going on?" he asked the two young women, sounding slightly out of breath.

"Oh, hi Peter," Kara said, smiling.

Charlynn greeted him, as well.

"Who was that man?" he asked in a hushed voice.

Kara frowned. "Man? What man?"

"It looked like you gave him several of my paintings just now."

The women looked at each other and then Kara laughed and said, "Oh, John? He does odd jobs for us. He's delivering some framed originals to a customer."

"You hire a homeless guy to deliver my art?" he asked, scolding.

"Oh," Kara said, "I thought you knew about him. Dawna said…"

"Yeah," Charlynn said, "he told us…"

Just then a woman's voice could be heard above the hum of the crowd. She was talking to a group of friends. "This is it! Look at this art. Just look at it. Isn't it fabulous? But you can't give it a quick look. You must spend time with it. This man has a lot to say and he says it brilliantly through his art. Let's go inside. I want to show you my favorite pieces," she said, pushing her way through to the gallery entrance.

Once they small group had walked past, Kara said quietly, "I'm sorry, Peter. I thought he worked for us."

"Where'd he go to…deliver the art?" he asked.

The two women looked at each other. Charlynn said, "Um, I think one of the office buildings around the corner."

He grimaced. "This time of night? What offices are open now? Did he pay for the art?"

"No, he said he'd give the checks and cash to Dawna after he collects."

Peter threw his hand up to his head and turned away. He spun back toward the two women. "And you believed him?" he said, trying to keep his voice down.

"Like I said, I thought you knew about him. I thought he worked for us," Kara repeated. She appeared to be near tears.

"Well, let's do this," Peter said. "Don't let anyone walk off with any of the art unless they've paid for it." He glared at the two women. "I can't even believe this," he said.

Charlynn frowned. "He was so convincing. Like Kara said, he's done jobs for us before. I thought that was how he earned his money."

***

As the group headed back toward the beach house an hour or so later, Iris said, "That was fun. I got a lot of ideas for home decorating."

"You enjoy home decorating?" Rochelle asked.

"Yes, other people's homes," she said. "Can't afford to do much to my own place."

"Yeah, she's too busy decorating her body with all those cool designer clothes she wears," Savannah said. "She helped me decorate our old turn-of-the-century home."

"Nice," Rochelle said. "I was into home decorating once."

"Is there any profession you haven't tried during your rather short time on this planet?" Savannah asked, chuckling.

Rochelle thought for a moment. "Yes, I've never been a hooker—the crocheting kind or the street kind."

Everyone laughed.

In the meantime, Craig caught up to Peter, who was walking alone since Rochelle had joined the women in conversation. "Hey Peter, I caught wind of something you might be interested in."

"Oh?" he glanced at Craig.

"Yeah, I overheard two guys talking about you... saying something about how someone is selling you out. One of them had evidently heard through what he considered a reliable source that you are going down."

Peter ran his hand through his hair. "Damn," he said. "Can you describe these men? Did they say anything more?"

"Naw, someone else walked up to them and they changed the subject. Yeah, I can describe them. Long hair, beards; one was turning grey. He wore shades, one was darker, wore a baseball cap. That one had some tats. One on his hand resembled Popeye."

"Popeye?" he questioned.

"Yeah, you know, the muscle-bound sailor who eats spinach? Or are you too young to know that character?"

"Where were these dudes?" Peter asked.

"On the beach side of a wall I was leaning against while Iris was looking at some of the trinkets along the promenade."

"Well, one of them might be the guy Charlynn gave those paintings to this evening, but I don't recall that he was wearing a baseball cap."

"What?" Craig asked.

Peter looked at the detective. "Oh nothing, really. Just thinking out loud. Hey, thanks for the heads-up. Sure isn't good to hear, but I need to know about it if I'm going to have to fight it. Just wish I knew what or who I'm fighting."

***

"I'll get her," Savannah said when she heard Lily fuss early the following morning.

"No, let me," Michael said, leaping out of the bed and heading toward the alcove.

"But I haven't gotten her up all week," she whispered, loudly.

"Neither have I," he said.

"Yes, you did. It's my turn," she complained.

Just then the door on the other side of the alcove opened a crack and Gladys asked, "Is everything all right?"

"Yes, Mom, we're just arguing over who gets to get Lily up this morning. You go back to bed and sleep in."

Gladys shook her head and grinned at her daughter and son-in-law.

An hour later, she joined them in the kitchen. "So, who won the argument?" Gladys asked, chuckling.

Savannah laughed. "We both did."

"How's that?" her mother asked.

Savannah said, "Michael got the first cuddle. I changed her and we took turns playing with her before breakfast."

"Yeah, watch this," Michael said. "She likes airplane kitty."

"Airplane kitty?" Gladys questioned.

Michael nodded. "Watch." He waved the baby's chenille cat in the air and made airplane noises, then crashed the kitty into her tummy and she giggled.

"Cute," Gladys said, laughing.

"But she likes tickle kitty more," Savannah said. "Wait 'til you see this." She took the stuffed cat from Michael and wriggled it against Lily's neck saying, "Tickle, tickle kitty."

Lily giggled.

"You two are silly," Gladys said, laughing. She walked past Lily, softly rubbing one hand over the baby's head, then poured herself a cup of coffee. "You're awake awfully early for people who've been staying up late every night."

"Yes, we kinda are, aren't we?" Savannah said. "Well, Iris and Craig have to leave this morning." She then suggested, "Hey Mom, how about taking a walk with me and Lily before the traffic gets heavy. Want to? Craig and Iris probably won't be up for another hour or so."

"On the beach?" she asked

"No, on the sidewalks. The stroller doesn't roll on the sand. You mentioned some of the gardens you've noticed. I'd like to take a closer look at them."

"That would be nice. Yes, let's do that." She turned to Michael. "Want to join us?"

"No, I think I'll walk up along the beach and get a paper, then read it out on the deck."

"Okay. I'll fix us some pancakes with blueberries when we get back." Savannah said, kissing Michael on the side of the head.

"Which way shall we go?" Savannah asked her mother as they stepped out to the sidewalk on the east side of the house.

"Let's go to the right. I think there's more to see that way."

After examining some of the most beautiful landscaping in the neighborhood, mother and daughter were just about ready to head back to the beach house when Savannah said, "That's where Peter's gallery manager lives—in the apartment up there."

"What's that noise, Vannie?" Gladys asked, as they got closer.

"Gosh, I don't know—like a motor running in the garage there." As they rounded the corner, Savannah began fanning her face. "Whew. There are fumes are coming from something. What is that?" she asked out loud, frowning.

"I don't know, but let's get the baby out of here," Gladys insisted.

Savannah wheeled past the apartment building as fast as she could toward Seahorse Street. Once they were half block away, Savannah stopped. She turned and looked back at the small apartment building. "Mom, I think something's wrong."

"Why, honey?"

"Well, it sounds to me like a car running in that garage. It's right below Dawna's apartment, so I imagine that's her garage. Even if it's not, you don't leave a car running in a closed up garage." She pushed the stroller toward Gladys. "Here, stay with Lily. I'd better check this out," she said, heading back up the street toward the apartments.

"Vannie, no. It could be dangerous," Gladys called after her. "No Vannie. Stay here, please."

*Sorry, Mom,* Savannah said to herself. *Something's terribly wrong and I have to find out what it is. Dawna could be in danger.* She sprinted to the large garage door and attempted to lift it. *Damn, must be automatic. Then there's another door,* she reasoned, rushing toward the stairs leading to Dawna's apartment. She stopped near the bottom of the staircase, *Good, a door with a window.* She peered in through the window. *It's dark. But I can see that there's a car in there and it looks like it's running. Good God.*

She tried the door knob. *Locked.* She looked around, hoping to see someone on the street who could help. That's when she spotted a flower pot sitting near the bottom step. She grabbed it and smashed it against the window; shards of glass scattered in all directions. *The fumes are awful,* she thought. She used the pot to remove the shards from the bottom of the window opening and reached in to unlock the door. *There's Dawna in the car. Dammit, what is she thinking?* "Dawna, Dawna—get out of there!" Savannah called. She then ripped off the sweatshirt she'd tied around her waist and wrapped it around her face. She started to dash into the garage, when she felt a hand on her shoulder.

"Stand back, ma'am," a man said, pulling her away from the door.

She turned and saw a large man rushing past her into the garage—a second man followed. Savannah stepped away from the garage and began to cough. When she spotted her mother with the baby half block away, she walked quickly toward them.

"Vannie, are you all right?" Gladys asked. "Thank heavens those men showed up."

"Yeah, where did they come from?" she asked, looking around.

"I guess they heard the commotion. I think they came out of the apartments there," Gladys said. "I called 9.1.1."

Savannah coughed and cleared her throat. "Oh good; I hear them coming."

"I called Michael, too," Gladys confessed.

The women watched from a distance as the two men opened the automatic garage door and carried Dawna out into the fresh air away from the fume-filled garage. They laid her on a patch of grass and one of them leaned over her.

"Looks like she's moving," Savannah said. "I'll be right back, Mom."

"Vannie, I'd rather you…" Gladys started.

But Savannah was not one to stand idly by. She walked swiftly to where the woman lay and knelt down next to the man. "Is she…?"

"She's still breathing," he responded without looking at Savannah.

"Dawna," she said, reaching out and shaking her by the shoulder.

Dawna groaned and rolled her head from side to side.

"Excuse me, ma'am," a paramedic said as he approached Dawna with an oxygen mask. Savannah stood and moved back a few feet. She watched as he fitted her with the mask and then began checking her over.

"What happened here?" a policeman asked Savannah.

"She was in the garage with the car running. I broke out the window and…" she looked around, "those men," she said, pointing, "went in and got her out of there."

"Savannah," Michael said, walking up to her. "What's going on?"

"Oh, Michael, Dawna was in the garage with the car running. She's been overcome by the fumes." She looked at Dawna as they put her on a stretcher. "Are they taking her to the hospital?" she asked the officer.

He nodded. He then focused on Savannah and asked, "Did you go inside the garage?"

"No. I started to, but those men showed up and pushed me away."

Michael took a deep breath and ran his hand through his hair. "Savannah, Savannah," he said shaking his head slowly.

Is she a friend of yours—a relative?" the officer asked.

"No," Savannah said, sheepishly. "I don't know her very well."

He looked carefully at her. "Are you feeling okay, yourself?"

"Yes, I'm okay," she said, continuing to glance in Dawna's direction. When Savannah saw that Dawna was being loaded into the ambulance, she started to walk toward her, but Michael took her arm and held her back.

"Let's go, hon," he said gently.

"But Michael…" Savannah protested, attempting to squirm away from her husband's grip.

"Step back," a policeman said to the small crowd that had gathered. "Give us room here."

"Okay," Savannah said, walking away with Michael toward the beach. "Let's stop in and tell Peter about this. He needs to know." She turned to her mother. "Mom, would you take Lily back to the house. We'll be there in a little while."

Several minutes later, the couple knocked on the back door of the gallery. "Who is it?" Peter called.

Michael responded. "Michael and Savannah."

"Hey, what are you doing out so bright and early?" Peter asked, after unlocking and opening the door.

Savannah cringed. "Bringing disturbing news, I'm afraid."

"What's happened?" he asked. "You look…well, kind of upset."

"Yes," she said. "Mom and I were walking with the baby and we found Dawna in the garage with the car running."

"What?" he said, looking confused. "Why would that be odd?"

"The garage was closed up. She was overcome by fumes."

Peter grabbed his head with his hands and looked up at the ceiling. "Good God," he said. He looked at Savannah and Michael. "Is she…?" he tried to ask.

Michael nodded. "She's alive. They took her to the hospital."

"Yeah, we really don't know her condition. But she is alive," Savannah confirmed.

Peter turned away, rubbing the back of his neck. "Why…? How…?" he started.

"I guess we won't know what happened until she can talk to someone," Savannah said. "Is Kara coming in today? I can stay here at the gallery if you want to go to the hospital," she offered.

His eyes darted as he tried to digest the news and figure out what to do. "No, I don't want you to do that," he said. "Yeah, Kara will be here later this morning. I'll just close up until then. It'll be okay," he said. He headed toward his office, then turned and walked up to Savannah and Michael. "Thanks for letting me know," he said, hugging Savannah. He squeezed Michael's shoulder. "Thanks, you two."

"Let us know what you find out, will you, Peter?" Savannah said, as the couple walked toward the back door.

"Sure will, guys. Thanks again."

***

"Had some excitement this morning, did you?" Craig asked, when he saw Savannah and Michael appear on the deck.

"Gladys told us about it," Iris said. "How is she?"

"How's Peter?" Craig asked.

"He's closing up shop to go see her at the hospital," Savannah explained. "As far as we know, she's alive. She was moving when they put her in the ambulance."

Iris glanced at her watch. "He opens his gallery this early?"

"Not usually. He was getting ready for his Sunday crowd. He opens around nine, I think, on Sunday." She focused on Iris and then Craig and asked, "So, do you have to leave this morning?"

"Yes, we need to get back to the real world," Iris said. "This has been so much fun. Thanks for sharing it with us."

"We're glad you could come," Savannah said.

"Did Peter say anything about what happened last night?" Craig asked.

"No, why?" Michael asked.

"Just wondering what he found out about the two guys I heard talking."

Savannah tilted her head. "What guys?"

"I'm guessing they were homeless. But I overheard them talking about Peter," he explained.

"Craig, was one wearing a baseball cap with some sort of little animal on the logo?"

Craig took a sip of coffee, then nodded. "Yeah, a fox or weasel," he said. "I didn't recognize the logo—probably some local business. Let me know what Peter finds out about him," he said. He then added, "Oh, and he had a Popeye tattoo on his hand."

***

201

It was after noon when Peter placed a call to Michael's phone. "Hi, Michael. Just wanted to let you know she's going to be okay. She says someone knocked her out and put her in the running car. Who would do that to her? I don't think she has any enemies of that caliber. Why would they do it?" he asked, not expecting an answer.

"Well, that *is* odd," Michael said. "Glad to hear she's going to be okay."

"Let me talk to Peter," Savannah said, reaching for the phone.

"Hi Peter. That's good news. How long will they keep her in the hospital?" she asked.

"Overnight, for sure. After that, I don't know. Depends on her condition, I guess."

"How is she…I mean mentally?" Savannah asked.

"Hard to tell," he said. "As I told Michael, she says someone did this to her."

"Oh!" Savannah exclaimed. "I thought…"

"Yeah," he said. "I think it is an obvious assumption that she would do this to herself. But she said some guy knocked her out and dragged her down to the garage and put her in the car. She didn't know anything until she woke up outside there on the grass with strangers around her."

"Can she have visitors?" Savannah asked, flatly.

"I guess," he said. "They didn't say anything to me about restrictions. Are you going to see her?"

"Yes, I'm thinking about it," she said. "Thanks for letting us know, Peter." She hesitated and then asked, "How are you?"

There was an exaggerated silence, and then, "Oh, I'm okay. Just a bit beaten down…know what I mean?"

"Yes, I think I do. Well, you take care. Be kind to yourself. See you later."

202

***

"Can't sleep, hon?" Michael asked later that night when he found Savannah wrapped in a blanket in a chair on the balcony. "Are you feeling okay?"

"Yeah, I'm okay," she said, reaching out her hand to him. He took it. "I just can't stop thinking about Dawna," she said, quietly. She looked up at Michael. "Why would she do this?"

Michael pulled a chair closer and sat facing Savannah. "She's troubled, honey. But didn't Peter say someone did this to her?"

"Yes, but I'm not sure I believe that. It seems far-fetched to me. I think she did this to herself. But why? She has a future. When I was with her the other day, she was talking about her future." Savannah looked Michael in the eyes. "Michael, I'm going to see her tomorrow."

Michael took in a deep breath and let it out.

"What? Don't you think I should?" she asked. Both of them were silent for a moment and then she said, "I feel responsible."

"What?" he almost shouted. He toned it down and said, "You feel responsible for what she might have done to herself? Why, for heaven's sake? That doesn't make any sense at all, Savannah."

"No," she said, chuckling. "I feel responsible for her life." She looked out over the ocean. "I can't explain it…but it was because of me that she didn't die. She either wanted to or someone else wanted her to…we don't know for sure. But she didn't die and it's because I found her. I don't know… there's a part of me that feels…well, responsible. I want to

203

see her. Maybe I need closure. I'm not sure, but I need to see her."

Michael ran his hand through his hair. "Okay, then. You should go see her, if they let you in—if *she* lets you in."

## Chapter 7

"Be careful," Michael said as Savannah prepared to leave in the car the following morning. "Traffic here is different than in Hammond. Do you remember how to use the GPS?"

"Yes, it still has the hospital address in it. I'll be fine. See you later, hon," she said, kissing him.

Thirty minutes later, Savannah walked up to the reception desk at the hospital. "Dawna…" she started to say to the receptionist, when she heard her name called. She turned. "Oh Peter, hello. How is she?" she asked.

He shook his head. "Not good," he said. When he saw Savannah turn glum, he said, "Oh, she's going to be okay physically, evidently, but otherwise she's a mess. Wouldn't even talk to me. Just kept crying."

Savannah grimaced. "Gosh, poor thing."

Peter frowned. "What are you doing here?" He glanced toward the elevators. "You didn't come to see her, did you?"

"Yes, actually, I did…But…"

"She may respond to you, you know?" Peter said. "She doesn't seem to have many friends."

"Well…I'll go in and see if she'll talk to me, then. I guess I sorta need…well, maybe closure. Some part of me needs to know she's all right."

Peter thought about that for a few moments, then said, "Savannah, can I talk to you?" He looked around and then led her to the waiting area. Once they were seated, he said, "You feel responsible, don't you?"

She looked surprised. "Well, yes." She hesitated, then asked, "Did you talk to Michael?"

He shook his head. "No, but I think I know what you're going through." He looked down at his hands. "I saved someone once who had tried to commit suicide." He looked off into space. "I dated her a few times and then moved on to another gal. I guess she thought we had a relationship. I was just into…you know…casual dating. Well, one night I ran into her at a club. Of course, I was with another woman. I didn't think much of it when she stormed out of the place, but when I got home, there was a message from her. It sounded…well, it made me head straight for her apartment." He paused. His voice cracked when he said, "I got there just in time. She had taken pills. They told me that a few minutes longer and it would have been too late." He looked at Savannah. "I know that feeling of responsibility. Because of me, she was alive even though she evidently wanted to be dead. But, of course, it was because of me that she wanted to be dead. So I had a double burden."

"Gosh, I guess you did," Savannah said. "So what did you do?"

"I started seeing her…but only as a friend. Something inside me needed to make sure she was okay. I took it upon myself to make her life better. I spent time with her. Made sure she ate. Took her places that I knew she enjoyed…things like that. She thought we were dating, and, I guess we kind of were. But my heart wasn't in it. I mean, I didn't have feelings for her outside of…well, obligation." He laughed. "Now how can you enjoy a relationship based on obligation?"

"But how does this relate to *my* going to see Dawna?" she asked.

He looked at her, studying her face. "Well, I guess it doesn't, really. My point in telling you this is to caution you to be careful. Don't get drawn into something that isn't right for you…that could interfere with or destroy your life."

"How could that happen? I just want to make sure she's okay and see if there's anything I can do to help," she said.

"Yes, I know. But someone who has the capacity for suicide…"

"We don't know for sure it was suicide, do we?" she asked. "Isn't it possible that the same person who stabbed her put her in the car?"

Peter was silent. He sighed deeply. "Interesting theory," he said, lowering his brows. He tilted his head. "You think this was attempted murder, do you?"

She shrugged. "Heck, I don't know. Could be, I guess."

"Who would want to do this? As I told Michael, I don't think she has any enemies."

Savannah opened her eyes wide before saying, "That man seemed to be angry with her the day we went for coffee."

He locked eyes with her. "Oh yes, you told me about that."

"He seemed to be stalking her. She was quite uncomfortable, but tried to brush it off, I think, for my benefit."

"Do you know who it was? Did she say anything about him?" he asked, obviously interested.

"No, only that…she hates homeless people."

He looked down at his hands. "The homeless, huh?" he said. He looked at her. "You know, your friend the detective was suspicious about a homeless guy the night we went on the art walk. I told him I'd see what I could find out about him. But I kinda forgot until now." He perked up. "Well, I'd better get to the gallery. Good luck with your visit," he said.

Savannah nodded. "Thanks. And thanks for the… warning." She lifted herself out of the chair and then turned and asked, "What room is she in?"

"Four-oh-four."

When Savannah stepped into the room, she saw Dawna lying on her back in the hospital bed, eyes closed. Savannah stopped just inside the door. *She looks so small in that bed…insignificant,* she thought. *Her aura of confidence seems to have drained from her.* Just then, Dawna opened her eyes. "Dawna?" Savannah said.

Dawna rolled her head in the direction of the voice. "Savannah," she said without emotion.

Savannah walked closer. "How are you feeling this morning?" she asked, trying not to sound too cheerful.

Dawna rolled her head back and forth on the pillow. "Okay, I guess." She looked at Savannah. "What are you doing here, anyway?"

Savannah put her hand on Dawna's arm. "I came to see you—wanted to make sure you're all right."

"I'm still here," she said rather sarcastically. She smirked and said more quietly, "…whether I want to be or not."

"So what happened?" Savannah asked. "Did someone…" she started.

"Dawna Paulson?"

The two women turned toward the sound of the voice and saw a man and woman standing just inside the doorway.

"Yes," Dawna said.

Savannah recognized the woman as Sergeant Markle from the police department and nodded to her.

The sergeant acknowledged Savannah and then walked toward Dawna, who had raised the head of her bed so she was sitting up straighter. "I'm Sergeant Markle and this is Detective Reed. We have a few questions, if you don't mind."

"Oh, God," she said. "What do you want to know?"

The sergeant glanced at Savannah, who said, "I can wait in the lobby."

"No," Dawna said. "I'd rather you stay, if you don't mind."

Savannah looked at the officers, who glanced at one another and silently agreed it was okay. She moved to the other side of the bed and leaned against the wide windowsill near a small stack of pillows and blankets.

"Ms. Paulson," the detective said, "can you tell us what happened yesterday?"

"Sure, I've been waiting to tell my story. Where have you damn cops been, anyway?" she snapped.

"Um, actually, Ms. Paulson," Sergeant Markle said, "we have your statement here. You spoke to officers after you were admitted yesterday. Don't you remember that?"

"No," she said, frowning. "Whatever I said yesterday isn't valid. That isn't a valid report," she insisted. "I didn't know what I was saying. I don't remember talking to any cops at any time until now."

"Okay," the sergeant said, "so what do you remember about what happened to you yesterday morning at your home?"

"Well," she said, eyes darting around the room, "a man dragged me out to my car and…knocked me out, and I guess he turned on the car and tried to kill me," she said.

"Can you describe the man?" Markle asked.

"Uh…he was probably one of the homeless. They're always hanging around."

"What did he look like?" the detective asked.

"He was grungy; had a beard and long hair."

"Were there any identifying marks or clothing?" he asked.

She thought. "Not that I can remember. But he got me out of bed, so I wasn't really wide awake."

The officers were silent and then the sergeant asked, "Did you sleep in your clothes that night?"

"Uh…" Dawna said. "Yeah, I guess I did." She chuckled and then began to babble. "Sometimes I do that. I'm so tired after my workday and then I paint some at night. I often go to bed fully dressed. Sometimes I don't even take my shoes off."

"Have you seen the man before?" Sergeant Markle asked.

Dawna hesitated, then said, "Oh, you mean the man who…? Uh…no, I don't think so. But they all look alike, you know."

The sergeant smirked. "Yeah, beard, long hair, grungy," she said, referring to her notes.

Dawna plopped her head back down on the pillow, closed her eyes, and said, "I don't think I can take any more right now. I'd like it if you'd leave."

The officers hesitated, then Detective Reed said, "Okay, we'll come back when you're feeling better."

Savannah watched as they left, then she stepped toward the bed and said, "I'd better be going, too."

"No," Dawna said, opening her eyes and lifting her head off the pillow. "Stay. I want to talk to you."

"Okay," she said, sounding a bit wary. She walked around to the other side of the bed and sat down in a chair. "Is that what really happened?" she asked. "It kind of sounded like you were either making it up or you were trying to protect someone."

Dawna's eyes flashed in anger. "What do you mean? That's what happened, dammit!"

Savannah sat quietly, watching Dawna. She then asked, "How long will they keep you?"

"I think I can go home today. The sooner the better. I have a lot to do."

"So what's on your agenda first?" Savannah asked, trying to make conversation. "What's the most important thing you want to do when they release you?"

Dawna laid back and looked out the window at the sky. "Paint," she said, thoughtfully. "I just want to paint."

"You sound like a woman with a passion."

"Oh yes. I thought my passion was Peter and his art. But now I've discovered that my passion is my own art."

"Do you have time to pursue your art?" Savannah asked.

"Yes. I paint at night in that storage unit I told you about. I converted it into my studio."

"Gads, Dawna, how do you work by day and paint at night?"

"Coffee and stay-awake pills," she admitted.

"No wonder you're so…energetic," Savannah said. "Do you ever let your system calm down?"

"No," she said. "I might fall asleep."

When Dawna noticed Savannah smiling at the irony of that comment, she began to chuckle.

"Good to see you still have a sense of humor," Savannah said. She leaned forward and asked, "Where do you see yourself in five years?"

Dawna adjusted the pillow under her head so she could look at Savannah. "Well, that's an off-the-wall question."

"Yes. Can you answer it? I think we all should be able to answer that question at any time. If we can't, something could be wrong with the way we're living—we are destined to fail. Some people have goals with no real direction and their life can be crap."

Dawna stared at Savannah. "You're talking about me, aren't you? You think my life is crap."

"I didn't say that."

The women were silent for a moment and then Dawna said, "My life *is* crap!"

Savannah grinned.

Dawna looked at her and her mouth turned up slightly. Tears filled her eyes, but she began to chuckle. Her chuckle turned into laughter. Soon both women were laughing.

"Why would you say that?" Savannah asked.

"Because I can't honestly answer your question."

"It's not really my question, is it? It's something you should be asking yourself."

Dawna thought about that statement for a moment and then said, "So true. Where do I see myself in five years? In the cemetery?"

"No, let's not go there. Come on, Dawna," Savannah urged.

"Okay," she said, dreamily. "In my own gallery selling my own art. That's where I'd like to see myself— traveling to shows all over." She spoke more quietly now. "I want Peter's life."

After a long silence, Savannah said, "That's a great goal, Dawna—and an honest one. Now, how do you plan to get there? What's the first step?"

"Oh," Dawna said, as if caught off guard, "that's an efficient way to approach it, isn't it? I've been so busy running around trying to do what I think I'm supposed to do that I never really stopped to think about how to achieve my goal."

"That not exactly true, Dawna," Savannah said. "You've been making preparations by staying awake at night painting. How many paintings do you have?"

"Dozens…maybe three dozen that are show-worthy."

"How long does it take you to create a painting?"

"Not long." Her eyes widened. "I can complete one in, say, two days. Sometimes less, sometimes more. It depends on the mood and the project."

"Pretty fast, then," Savannah said. "I'd like to see your art."

Dawna looked at her. "Really?"

"Yes. After they spring you, let me know when you're going to your…studio again and I'll go with you."

Dawna smiled. "Okay. I'd like that."

"Do you need anything?" Savannah asked.

Just then a doctor walked in. "Dawna Paulson?" he asked.

"Yes," Dawna said, cringing a little.

He looked down at her chart. "How are you feeling?"

"Pretty good," she said. "Can I go home?"

"Well, let's see," he said, proceeding to examine her. When he finished, he looked at her chart again. "I can't see any reason to keep you. You didn't breathe in too much carbon monoxide. I hear the windows on the car were rolled up and the fumes were mostly outside the car—filling the garage. You probably don't have any rats or mice in that garage, though," he said with a chuckle.

Savannah noticed that Dawna didn't seem to appreciate the doctor's attempt at humor. She addressed him, "I can take her home. Is the paperwork ready?"

He thought for a moment, then responded, "Yeah, I'll take care of it." He glanced at his patient. "I imagine she'll be ready to go in thirty minutes or so."

***

While Savannah waited in the lobby with a cup of coffee, she called Michael to let him know she'd be delayed. In the meantime, Dawna took a shower and freshened up. An hour later, she directed Savannah to her studio in the storage unit.

"Here it is—no windows. It's quiet. I sometimes paint wearing ear buds and listening to classical music," she explained. She used a key to unlock the padlock, opened the door, and turned on the light.

Savannah's eyes were immediately drawn to a painting in progress on an easel. "Dawna," she said, walking toward it, "this is lovely." She looked around at other paintings that were leaning against the walls and lying on a long table. "She glanced from one area of the room to another, examining the artwork "Well, you are versatile."

Dawna smiled.

"Look at this; it's quite similar to Peter's style, isn't it?"

Dawna moved in front of that group of paintings and pointed Savannah in another direction. "Yeah, I can paint like he does, but I'm not in love with that style. I prefer this," she said, pointing out a group of three paintings.

"Gosh, they're so light and free and…well, just lovely," Savannah said. "I don't think I've ever seen anything quite like it, except maybe in high-class home-furnishing stores. It's so conducive to the home environment—as opposed to banks or that type of thing. This is private art, not public art." She looked at Dawna, who was smiling.

"I'd love to get in with a home-furnishing company. That would be my goal for…maybe six or seven years from now," she said. Suddenly, she looked at her watch. "Hey, I'd really like to make a few phone calls. Do you mind taking me home?" She crinkled up her nose. "I want to change out of these clothes—they stink."

"Sure, I'll drive you home," Savannah said. "Hey, thanks for showing me your studio. I'm impressed. Dawna, I'd really like to see you take the steps toward following your dream. There's no reason for you to continue helping Peter pursue his, is there? Isn't it time for Dawna to shine?" She turned to leave with Dawna when she suddenly stopped. "What?" Dawna asked, when she saw the look on Savannah's face.

Savannah pressed her lips together and said, "I have an idea. I'll check back with you later."

It was close to noon when Savannah walked into the beach house and found Michael and her mother on the deck playing a card game. "Hi guys," she said, joining them.

"Hi, how is she?" Michael asked.

"She's okay," Savannah said, dropping into a chair at the table where the couple sat.

"Then what took you so long?" he asked.

"Just girl stuff," she said. "Lots to talk about."

Just then, Peter appeared from the beach wearing

board shorts, flip-flops, and a t-shirt. "Hi all," he said, cheerily.

"No work today?" Michael asked.

"Yeah, I worked this morning. Kara and Charlynn are at the gallery now. I thought I'd take some time off this afternoon." He looked at Michael. "Wanna go surfing?"

"Surfing, you say? Me?"

"Come on. I know you used to surf. Did you forget how?"

"Gosh, I hope not." He looked from Savannah to Peter. "Do you have a board I can use?"

"Yup—in the garage."

"An extra wet suit?"

"Yup."

"Well, then, I guess I don't have an excuse." He looked out at the waves. "They don't look too brutal today. Yeah, let's try it." To Savannah and her mother, he added, "You ladies want a good laugh? Just stay out here and watch me try to remember how to surf." He headed for the house, shaking his head and mumbling. "Surfing…at my age? Am I crazy or what?"

"Peter," Savannah said, once Michael had disappeared into the house, "can I talk to you?"

"Sure," he said, sitting down across from her at the table.

"Oh, there's the baby," Gladys said, picking up the baby monitor. "I'll get her."

Peter watched as Gladys disappeared into the house, then looked Savannah in the eyes and said, "Thanks for taking care of Dawna today. She seems to have calmed down quite a bit."

"You talked to her?" she asked.

"Yes, on the phone. She seems…happier today."

"Well, that's what I want to talk to you about. Peter, have you seen her art?"

Peter looked confused. "Well, she showed me pictures of some of it when we first met. Why?"

"She has a whole studio full of wonderful art."

"She does?" he asked, furrowing his brow.

"Yes, she's been painting at night and I think it's really good stuff. I was just wondering if you could possibly give her a show at your studio some evening."

He sat silent for a few moments, obviously digesting Savannah's idea. Finally, he responded. "Uh, gosh, I don't know."

"It would help her, I think. She has dreams like you did and she doesn't quite know how to launch them into reality."

"What are you talking about? She's the most confident woman I know."

"Peter, she craves to be known as an artist. She wants to live your life. I'd like to suggest that you let her have a show in your gallery. What do you think?"

He sat back in his chair and ran his hand over the back of his neck. "Gosh, I can't think of any reason why not, but are you sure she wants that?"

"Ask her, would you? Just ask her."

"Okay," he said. "I will."

"Ready?" Michael asked as he returned wearing his board shorts.

Peter took one more look at Savannah and then said to Michael, "Yes. Come on, I'll show you where the boards are. You can have your pick."

"Be careful, hon," Savannah called after her husband.

***

Two afternoons later, Savannah and Michael walked to the gallery. When they entered, they saw Peter and Kara busily helping Dawna hang her paintings.

"You do some beautiful work," Kara said, standing back and looking at a panel of the art. "They would make really great note cards, too."

Peter nodded. "Yes they would." He looked at Dawna and said, "I had no idea. Why didn't you tell me?"

"Oh, I don't know. I guess I thought you'd..." she started. Suddenly, she noticed Savannah. She rushed to her, hugging her tightly. "Thank you," she said, choking up a little. She pulled back and looked into Savannah's eyes. "Peter said this was your idea."

"Well...uh...I..." Savannah stuttered.

"Thank you so much," Dawna said, hugging her again.

Savannah smiled. "Sure." She then held Dawna at arm's length and asked, "Hey, how're you feeling?"

"I feel wonderful," she said. "I'm so excited."

Savannah studied the woman. "Well, you look fabulous. She glanced around the room. "Now where are the refreshments? I'm in charge of refreshments."

"Everything's set up just around the corner," Dawna said. "But there's no need for you to hide out in there until we open. We're still hanging the art. Just browse and enjoy."

"These are really nice," Michael said, perusing the artwork. Different from Peter's, but attractive art."

"Thank you," Dawna said, with a smile and a slight bow.

Half hour later, Peter opened the doors to the public. The atmosphere was festive, with free-flowing champagne served in crystal glasses and a variety of attractive finger foods. The crowds were constant and jovial and Dawna's art was selling.

About halfway through the evening, a woman walked up to Peter and said, "This looks familiar; I've seen it in here before, haven't I?"

Peter shook his head. "No, this is the artist's first showing. It's nice, isn't it?"

The woman looked more closely at the paintings.

Just then a man said to her, "We have one real similar to this. Hung it in our bathroom."

Savannah had overheard the man's comments. "Oh, that would be good in a bathroom, with the right color scheme." She turned to the man and asked, "Where did you get yours?"

"Right in here," he said. "My wife and I walked in one afternoon and found it."

Peter said, "Oh you must be mistaken. You're seeing this art for the first time."

"Who's the artist of your piece?" the woman asked the man.

"I don't recall," he said. "Must be confused about where I bought it, though." He looked around. "Sure thought it was here."

Just then, Peter saw another local gallery owner walk in and he excused himself, saying to the potential customers, "Enjoy the evening. The violinist will start playing in a few minutes." He pointed. "Refreshments are around the corner." He then greeted the new guest. "Hi, Sean. How's it going?"

"Good. Thought I'd come down and see what all the commotion's about. You have standing-room-only outside there." He glanced out the window. "...or, sitting room..."

he said. "Nice touch, putting tables and chairs out in front. Did the city authorize that?"

"Yeah, of course," Peter said, laughing.

"So Dawna is showing her stuff, tonight, huh?" Sean asked.

"Yes, come in and take a look. The woman's got talent. She'll probably open her own gallery and put both of us out of business," Peter said, chuckling.

Sean stepped toward the exhibits. He squinted at the paintings and said, "I've seen her work before, but I didn't know it was *your* Dawna's."

"Really?" Peter said. "Where?"

"Some guy brought one to me for framing. He said he bought it unframed because it was cheaper and then couldn't find a frame that showed off the piece right, so he came to me." Sean turned to Peter. "You don't do framing, right?"

"Not after the fact and not for walk-ins," he said. "But where did the guy get Dawna's art? I thought this was her first show."

Sean shook his head. "I guess not," he said. "It was definitely one of hers."

***

"Tonight's sales came to $6,525.35," Kara reported to the small group that had stayed to help clean up after the show.

"Wow!" Dawna said, swooning a little. "I'm so stoked. What an evening." Turning to Savannah and Peter, she said, "Thank you." Before they could respond, she acknowledged Michael and Kara, as well, "Thank you all for making this possible."

"Congratulations, girl," Peter said, pulling Dawna to him and hugging her tightly. "You deserve it. Your stuff's good." He stepped back and asked her, "Now what?"

Dawna glanced from Peter to Savannah. "I'd like to…you know…pursue my own art," she said pouring her second—or third—glass of champagne.

"Well, I don't want to lose you. Do you think you could continue to run my business—do my bookings and all—and promote your art at the same time?"

"Really?" Dawna said. "You don't think that would be a conflict of interest?"

"No," Peter said. "It would be giving a leg-up to another artist, like a man named Henry Barton did for me many years ago. Just tell me what kind of help you need here and I'll hire an assistant for you—someone to do the books, make the calls, fill out the forms…you can handle the promotion and negotiations and that would free you up to promote your own work, as well. I can see it working out, can't you?"

Dawna stared at Peter. Suddenly, she turned and darted through the back of the gallery and out the door into the alley.

"What did I say?" Peter asked, obviously stunned.

Savannah cringed. "I don't know for sure, but I have a sneaking hunch. I'll see if I can talk to her," she said, grabbing her jacket and heading after her.

"Not alone, you're not," Michael said, following along behind his wife.

"Where'd she go?" Savannah asked, as the couple looked around. "There," she said, walking toward the sound of a woman weeping. They discovered Dawna slumped over in front of a parked car. "Dawna, what's wrong?" Savannah asked.

"Go away. I should never have agreed to this," she said.

"What are you talking about? You were a smashing success and so was your art."

"Yeah, and Peter had to go and spoil it all," she wailed.

"How did he do that? I thought his offer was fair and it gives you time to pursue your art."

Dawna continued to cry.

"What are you afraid of, success?" Savannah asked.

"Nooo," Dawna said. "It's Peter. How could he… after all I've done to him."

"How could he what?" Savannah asked.

"How could he…sniff, sniff…be so niiiiice," she wailed.

Savannah looked at Michael. He raised his eyebrows and shrugged. She sucked in air, then reached out and took Dawna by the shoulders. "Okay, kiddo, time to come clean."

"Huh?" she said. "What are you talking about?"

"I want to know what *you're* talking about. There's something more you have on your conscience, isn't there, Dawna? Come on; out with it. You'll never get that opportunity you want if you don't clean the slate."

Dawna took a ragged breath and blotted her face with a tissue. She ran one index finger around her eyes, trying to wipe away any mascara smears. After sipping again from the champagne glass she still held in one hand, she started to speak. Suddenly something caught her eye and she called out, "Hello, kitty. Here kitty-kitty," she said, slurring her words a little. "Come here. You could probably use a handout. You and me, we're both friendless in California—or will be as soon as the truth comes out." She took another swig of champagne. "Come here, kitty. Tell me your secrets and I'll tell you mine."

Savannah and Michael peered in the direction Dawna was looking, wondering what she saw there. After a couple of moments, Savannah shouted. "Rags! Michael, it's Rags!"

He blinked, disbelieving. "Good lord, big boy, what are you doing here?"

Dawna looked up at the couple. "That's your cat? I thought it was a…what do ya call it…" she said, swaying a little. "…a stray cat. I swear I've seen him out here before… right in the alley here."

Savannah said, "Well, we did walk up here with him once."

"Nope," Dawna said. "He was all by himself and alone."

Savannah looked at Dawna. "He's been to your house, you know."

Dawna squinted in the cat's direction and said, "Oh yes, he did come to my house that night I…was stabbed."

Michael scooped the cat up in his arms, saying, "I'll take him inside."

"Hey, what did you do, go home and get your cat?" Peter asked, laughing, when he saw Michael walk in.

Michael shook his head and set Rags down on the floor. "No, he showed up on his own."

Just then Dawna appeared with Savannah, who was carrying Dawna's champagne glass. "Dawna, are you all right?" Peter asked. "What happened? What did I say?"

She eased herself into a chair, rested her head in her palms for a moment and then sat upright. "Peter," she said, "I have a confession. In fact, dammit, I have several confessions."

"What are you talking about?" he asked.

"Just shut up and listen, will ya?" she said, still slurring some of her words. "I'm only going to say this once to you and, I guess," she said more quietly, "one more time to the police…" her voice trailed off.

As Dawna spoke, Rags sat at Michael's feet staring at the distraught woman. She looked down at him. "You know the truth, don't you, cat? He's seen a lot and heard a lot." She turned to Savannah. "This isn't the first time he's wandered down here by himself. I just didn't know it was your cat," she said, glancing at Michael and then back at Savannah.

"What does Rags know, Dawna?" Savannah asked gently.

"Peter, I'm the one who's been messing things up around here. I tried to keep you out of the shows. I hired people to damage your paintings and toss them into the Dumpster out there. It's all me."

Peter stood stunned. He glared down at Dawna. Finally, he asked, his voice weak, "Why?"

Dawna spoke slowly and deliberately. "I wanted you to go down…don't you see? I didn't know how to promote myself *and* you!" She shouted, "The only way I could get my success was to ruin you!" She sobbed into her hands and then said quietly, "Then you were nice." She looked up at him, her eyes filled with tears, mascara streaking down her cheeks. "Don't you understand? It's the only way I could see to do it."

Peter began to pace. He stopped in front of her. "You tried to damage my reputation? It was you?" He shook his head. "I thought you were the only one I could trust."

"That's right, Peter," Dawna said, "get mad. Get real mad. Maybe it'll make me feel better. I didn't know. I just didn't know any other way."

"So you manipulated, schemed, and lied!" he shouted, still pacing back and forth in front of her. He stopped, took hold of her shoulders, and made her look into his face. "What about the stabbing attack and the…incident in the garage?"

Dawna grimaced, her lips quivering. "There was no attack. I staged those things."

"Why?" he asked, loudly.

"'Cause I'm a drama queen," she said, laughing amidst tears. She looked at Peter, Michael, and Savannah and then down at the cat. "He knows," she said, pointing at Rags, who was now lying in his Egyptian-cat pose. "I stabbed myself and I tried to gas myself. It was all me."

"Why?" Peter asked, the pain in his heart showing clearly on his face.

"I wanted to die. But more than that, I wanted to make a statement. I wanted to be noticed. At times, my dreams seemed unreachable—that was unbearable! Do you understand?" she shouted. "Unbearable!" She then spoke more softly. "And I didn't want to face the things I had done."

"Face what?" he asked, running his hand through his hair.

"Oh, jail; your wrath…"

"Who was going to tell?" he asked. "I certainly didn't know what was going on."

"Those men I hired, maybe. It would be revealed; it was just a matter of time. I was making mistakes." She became agitated again and began to speak faster. "I wanted to stop…was in too deep. Peter, I was tired…tired of living this lie of a life.”

“Dawna,” Savannah asked, somberly, “did you try to poison Peter?”

She looked at Savannah and nodded. “Yeah. Failed at that, too.”

“You nearly killed our dog!” she shouted.

Michael reached out and grabbed Savannah’s arm, pulling her back.

“Well, she did,” Savannah said, crossing her arms in front of her.

Dawna looked at Savannah and Michael only briefly and then sobbed into her hands. “I’m sorry. I really am sorry. I made a mess of everything.”

“Dawna, what you’ve done is illegal,” Peter said.

“What are you going to do?” she asked, sniffling.

He paced back and forth in front of her. “I don’t know. I just don’t know. Right now, I’d like to be alone.” He looked around at everyone. “Let’s lock up and go home.” He glanced at Dawna. “We’ll load your paintings in the morning.”

Dawna continued to sit and stare at the floor in front of her, until Savannah knelt down next to her. “Dawna, Michael and I’ll walk you home. Will you be okay by yourself tonight?”

She nodded.

“I’m serious, Dawna,” Savannah said, sternly. “I want your promise that you won’t do anything stupid. I want you to get in bed and try to get some sleep. We’ll meet you here in the morning, say eight…?” she looked at Peter. He nodded. “Dawna, do you promise?” she asked.

The distraught woman looked at Savannah. “I promise,” she said, weakly.

226

"I believe you," Savannah said. "Now let's go, shall we?"

Michael picked up the cat and the trio walked a half block out of their way to make sure Dawna got home okay. Then they walked back to the beach house, which they found dark, except for a small porch light. After letting themselves in, Savannah turned on a light and Michael tossed the cat out in front of them. Rags scurried off toward the kitchen.

***

The following morning the fog hugged the coastline, so the Iveys opted to have coffee inside. Michael fed Lily her breakfast while Savannah used the last of the bread and eggs to make French toast. Suddenly, they heard a rap on the door.

"Hi, come on in," Michael said, when he opened the door and saw Peter standing there. "You look like you could use a cup of coffee and maybe breakfast," Michael offered as he ushered his friend into the kitchen. "Savannah's making French toast. We have some of that blueberry topping you like."

"Sounds good," Peter said, without much enthusiasm.

"Morning," Savannah said when Peter appeared in the kitchen. She asked in a serious tone, "How are you, this morning?"

"Well, I'm not sure. Still reeling from that wallop I got last night." He shook his head. "Man, I didn't see that coming."

Michael looked down at his feet. "Yeah, it was quite a blow." He then looked Peter in the eyes and asked, "Do you know what you're going to do?"

Savannah handed Peter a cup of coffee and he sat down. He smiled at Lily for a moment and then cleared his throat. "I talked it over with Rochelle…" He looked up at the two of them and grinned. "She's an amazing woman, you know it?"

Michael and Savannah exchanged glances. Michael said, "So, you've found a keeper there, huh?"

"I hope so," Peter said with a deep sigh. As for Dawna…poor, poor, Dawna…I think she's got herself all mixed up inside. I don't know if it's drugs or depression or what it is, but it appears that she's one sick woman. She needs help. Rochelle made some recommendations that I'm going to talk to Dawna about today."

Savannah frowned. "Do you think she'll seek help?"

Peter straightened. "It's either that or she'll have to deal with the authorities." When no one commented, he said more quietly, "If she gets help, I may consider sponsoring her within the art community. In the meantime, I have some resumes on file for her position and I will start interviewing."

"Have you talked to Dawna this morning?" Savannah asked.

"Yes, I called her. We're meeting later today."

"Oh, I told her I'd help load up her art this morning," Michael said.

"No hurry. I'm closing the gallery today. I'll help her pack it up after our meeting."

"If you need my help, just call," Michael offered.

"Do you have a bead on the man who was helping Dawna?" Savannah asked. "It was probably the one I kept seeing around the gallery."

"No," he said. "I don't think I'll go after him. It appears that he was acting on Dawna's orders. Without her,

I doubt he's a threat." He looked up from his coffee cup and added, "…but if he keeps showing his face around my place, I will take action." He looked at Michael and then Savannah. "So when are you heading home?"

"Sadly, tomorrow," Savannah said. "Peter, I…we…can't thank you enough for…"

"Aw, cut it out," Peter said. "As I said, you guys being here meant more to me than you can ever imagine." He stood up and enveloped Savannah in a bear hug. "Thank *you*," he said. He pulled away and looked into her eyes, "…from the bottom of my heart." He turned to Michael and held out his arms, inviting a hug, then slapped Michael on one shoulder and clasped his right hand around Michael's. Laughing, he said, "And thank you, you old nag doctor." When he started to feel himself choking up, he knelt down to the baby's level and began playing peek-a-boo with her. Once he had her laughing, he rubbed her head, stood up, and said, "She is some cute kid." Just then, he noticed Gladys enter the room. Peter smiled, saying, "And it all started with this beautiful woman."

"Huh?" Gladys said, her brown eyes dancing in response to the compliment.

"Well, the way I see it, you're responsible for this cute kid. It all started with you, right?"

"Oh, absolutely," she said, smiling.

Peter then suggested, "Well, if this is your last night, how about we barbecue? I'll bring the steaks."

Michael and Savannah looked at one another and she said, "Yeah, let's do that. I'll make a kale salad. Mom will you make your smashed potato salad again?"

"Sure," she agreed. "And we can cook up some of Grandma's chili beans."

"Will you bring Rochelle?" Savannah asked Peter.

"I hope so," he said, smiling.

***

That evening, Peter and Rochelle arrived, steaks in hand. Rochelle had made guacamole. Once everyone was comfortable on the deck around the fire pit, Savannah asked, "Peter, how did it go with Dawna today?"

"She was not happy, but she agreed to my terms."

"She'd be a fool not to," Michael said. "So you moved all of her art?"

"Yes. Didn't take long." Peter took a sip of sangria and then added, "Hey, an interesting thing happened at the gallery." When he had everyone's attention, he continued, "This guy walks in with a painting and asks me to sign it. I was surprised, but once in a while one gets past me without being signed—especially some of my earlier stuff that shows up when I least expect it. Well, so I take a better look at this painting and realize it isn't one of mine, and I tell the man so. He insists that he bought it in the gallery. Dawna was still there gathering her things and when he saw her, he identified her as the one who sold it to him."

Peter took a breath. "I asked her if she knew anything about it and what she told me blew me away. Come to find out, Dawna painted it. It looked so much like my work, I almost didn't know the difference," he said.

"So why was she copying your work?" Rochelle asked. "I thought she had a totally different style."

"That's right. But it seems that whenever I was out of town, she would bring her work in and sell it, hiding mine. She led with work that looked like mine—you might say they were knock-offs—so our regular customers wouldn't be suspicious."

"Gosh, I didn't see any of those paintings in her studio," Savannah said. She raised a finger in the air, saying, "Wait a minute. I did see a painting I thought was yours, but she steered me away from it right away." She shook her head slowly, muttering, "Unbelievable."

Peter said, "She is one calculating woman, I'll tell you…"

"Gosh, I guess. She thought of every angle, didn't she?" Savannah said.

Peter agreed. "Just about."

"Can you have her arrested for that?" Michael asked.

"If she'd forged my name, maybe. Otherwise, I don't know. But the woman sure made some money off those knock-offs. Remember how I complained on those days when she told me sales were down—always when I was out of town? Well, she was selling her work and racking up the bucks." He took a sip of sangria.

Everyone sat with their own thoughts for a moment, then Savannah said, "Peter, I have a question."

"Shoot," he said.

"Remember the night we went to the charity show?"

"Yeah."

"I saw Kara and Charlynn that night, and it seemed as though they were involved in something—well, I don't know—clandestine, I guess."

"How so?" Peter asked, lowering his brows.

"Well, they were hiding in some bushes and it looked as though they were spraying paint all over a painting. They tossed it and the can of paint into the bushes and ran off laughing."

Peter smiled.

"So do you know what they were up to?"

He nodded. "Yeah. It was part of a mystery the program director designed. Attendees were supposed to solve the mystery using clues found throughout the grounds. Kara and Charlynn got roped into helping with that game. I donated one of my paintings to the winner."

"Oh," Savannah said. "I thought…"

"What?" Peter asked, "…that the girls were involved in trying to take me down?" He laughed. "Not hardly." He sucked in a breath and said, "But I didn't think Dawna would, either…"

"So how do you feel now about helping her get started in the business?" Savannah asked.

"Interesting you should ask," Peter said, taking Rochelle's hand and smiling at her. "I've made some new decisions. I'm leaving the beach gallery and moving my action up north."

"Really?" Michael said.

"Yes. I think I'll open a gallery in Frisco. I'm ready for a big city and Rochelle's coming with me," he said, looking around at the others for their reactions.

"Wow! That's big," Savannah said. "Quite a change." She looked at Rochelle and then back at Peter. "Congratulations, you two."

"Yes, I realize I've been coasting in this laid-back environment. This…fiasco has spurred me on to become more aggressive in my approach to my work—and maybe be more hands-on and less…trusting."

"Will you sell the beach property?" Savannah asked.

Peter grinned at her. "Why, you want to buy it?"

"I wish," she said. "But no. Just wondering."

"I'm not sure. I'll probably keep it." He squeezed Rochelle's hand. "We do love the beach. And I have friends here. It would be nice to have it to come back to. I still may do shows in LA."

Savannah addressed Rochelle: "So, Rochelle, how does Peter's aura look now?"

"Bright and shiny," she said, smiling. "Like a new penny."

"A penny? Is that all?" Peter asked.

Savannah and Rochelle laughed.

Rochelle said, "And he has started the process of letting Dawna go."

"Oh?" Savannah questioned.

Peter nodded. "Yes. Just like the rest of us, she has choices. It's up to her to make the best ones for herself. I'm not responsible. You, Savannah, are not responsible. Her life is up to her."

"Amen," Savannah said. "That must feel good."

"Huh?" Peter said.

"To release that burden," she explained.

"Oh, yes. It sure does," he said. He looked from Savannah to Michael. "So you're heading back up north tomorrow?"

The couple nodded. She said, "Our wonderful dream vacation is almost over."

"Yeah, your calm, quiet, no-stress vacation…" Peter said, winking.

Everyone laughed.

"So what awaits you at home?" Rochelle asked. "Anything interesting?"

"Probably a few ailing dogs, cats, hamsters, and horses," Michael said. "And I want to finish up Adam's new bedroom when we get back."

"What awaits me is an orchard full of fruit I need to can," Savannah said. "I can't wait to catch up with our friends and family—maybe we'll invite them all over for a night of home movies." She laughed.

"Of your vacation?"Peter asked. He snickered. "It would be more like an Alfred Hitchcock movie."

"That's right," she said. She leaned forward. "Oh, and the premiere of Rags's documentary is scheduled in a few weeks in San Francisco, so maybe we'll run into you two up there."

"How exciting," Rochelle said. "Will Rags be there?"

"Yeah, he's already wearing his ash-colored tuxedo," Peter said, laughing out loud.

Michael shook his head and took a deep breath. "We haven't decided about that. Of course, Rob, the director, wants us to bring him. But you've seen how high-maintenance he can be."

"Oh, you've gotta bring him," Peter said. He looked at Rochelle. "Yeah, I hope we're up there by then. It would be a kick to see that documentary."

Rochelle nodded.

Just then, Savannah recognized the sound of the ringtone on her cell phone. She picked it up and looked at it. "Well, I'll be," she said. "It's Rob. Hi Rob," she said into the phone, as she walked away from the group to talk.

When she returned, she said, "The second Saturday night in July at the investor's home near Frisco. We'll make sure you get an invitation."

"But this time," Michael said, grinning at Peter, "would you keep the drama level down? Let's have a nice, quiet weekend, shall we?"

"Uh-oh," Peter said, pointing toward the edge of the deck, "you'd better issue the same warning to your cat."

"Excuse me. Is this your cat?"

Michael and Savannah twisted toward the voice and were shocked to see a security guard standing there, holding Rags in his arms. "Yes," Michael said, his brows creased. "Where…? How…?" he started.

The guard stepped up onto the deck as Michael walked toward him, reaching out for the cat. "Well, you see, sir, he wandered into Rudy's Fish Place and was evidently bothering the diners. Someone there recognized the cat and sent me up here with him."

"Oh my gosh, that's a first," Savannah said, feeling a sense of panic. "Where is this place?"

"Across town," he pointed, "—say a mile or so. Someone saw him climb off a bus just outside the restaurant."

Michael's jaw dropped. "What?"

In the meantime, Peter and Rochelle sat stunned.

"He rode a bus?" Michael asked, disbelieving. "He's never done that before. How did he…?"

Savannah walked up to Michael and put her hand on his arm. Looking sheepish, she said, quietly, "Well, yes, he has ridden a bus before." She winced. "Haven't I told you that story?"

Michael shook his head. "Honey…you've gotta be kidding me. The cat has a bus pass?"

"Yeah, I guess he does," she said. "He rides for free." She petted Rags as Michael held him, and then glanced up to see everyone looking at her, waiting to hear the story. "Well, when I lived in LA, I used to take him for walks. When I wanted to go over to Mom's or one of us got tired of walking, we'd sometimes get on a bus. He loved riding the bus. So one day, we get on the bus and the driver tells me that he had taken Rags for a ride by himself a few times."

"Oh my gosh," Rochelle said. "Where did he go?"

"Well, one time, he just rode the bus through the route and when they came back to the stop close to our place, the driver booted him out. Oh yes," she said, "he knows how to ride a bus."

By then, Peter and Rochelle were bent over laughing. The security guard attempted to stifle his amusement.

Savannah continued, "So this evening, he may have hopped on a bus at the corner and ridden for a ways. When he smelled the aroma of fish frying, he decided to get out and investigate. Gosh," she said, shaking her head. "I haven't thought about that in a long time. I would never have guessed he'd…"

"But he's not supposed to be getting out at all," Michael said. "He has evidently found a way." He addressed the cat, saying, "Sorry, buddy, but tonight, you're sleeping in the big cage." He walked into the house with Rags and disappeared.

The security guard took off his hat and rubbed one hand over his balding head. "Well, if that don't beat all," he said. "I've had a lot of experiences on this job, but never a bus-riding, escape-artist cat." He turned to leave. "Well, thanks for the chuckle," he said, as he stepped down off the deck.

"And thank you for bringing him back," Savannah called.

Once Michael had joined the others for one last good-bye, Peter said, "What an entertaining evening. Hey, you've *gotta* bring Rags to Frisco. He'll steal the show."

"And everything else that's not nailed down," Michael said. "I don't know, gang. It's a big responsibility taking him anywhere. Lily has better manners."

236

"But yeah," Savannah said. "He'll probably be with us. It *is* his movie debut, after all."

Additional books in the Klepto Cat Mystery series:

**Catnapped (Book One)**
When Savannah Jordan agrees to help her aunt while she recovers from a broken foot, she doesn't expect to walk into a mystery, become part of a not-quite-legal surveillance team, be kidnapped by a deranged stranger and meet a steaming hot veterinarian.

Beloved neighborhood cats are missing—the community can only guess at their fate—and Aunt Margaret's life is being threatened. Is it because she has a clue to the missing cats or is it something more sinister? Of course, as in all of the Klepto Cat Mysteries, Rags, an ordinary cat with a most unusual habit, has a paw in saving the day.

If you like light mysteries with only a little terror, if you're infatuated by interesting cats and if you love a love story, you must read this book.

**Cat-Eye Witness (Book Two)**
Savannah and Aunt Margaret open the old Forster home to the Hammond Cat Alliance for a fundraiser to help rehabilitate the abused horses rescued months earlier from the catnappers.

Before the afternoon is over, the collected funds go missing and someone is murdered in an upstairs bedroom.

Suspicion surrounds Iris, a local waitress and Savannah's new best friend. The only witness to the murder is Rags, Savannah's cat. With the assistance of a cat psychic and Rags's good friend, Charlotte (the young girl with

Downs), the cat helps to "paw" the killer…but not before an attempt is made on Rags's life. The case is solved only after Rags comes face-to-face with the killer for the second time.

Detective Craig Sledge is new to this book, as is Damon, Iris's errant son. Sledge finds this to be one of the muddiest cases he has ever worked, with inconsistent clues and no apparent motive. He's constantly surprised, perplexed, and impressed by the cat's uncanny ability to come up with clues he has missed. His fascination with the attractive Iris Clampton also mystifies the detective.

In this story, one of the rescued horses goes into labor and there's a night of high drama at the ole corral as veterinarians Savannah and Michael work to save the foal. This experience renews Savannah's deep interest in horses and riding, which ultimately serves to help her bond with a very important surprise character who finds his way into her life and Michael's just as they prepare to say their wedding vows.

While Rags is the animal star, he isn't the only animal featured in this story. Layla is back in all of her tangerine feline beauty. And Rags makes friends with Buffy, a perky almost Himalayan cat and the inseparable duo, Walter, an all black cat and his sidekick, Lexie, a charming Afghan-mix dog. Savannah's new ride, Peaches, also debuts in this story. An incident with this mare adds another dimension to Savannah's and Michael's relationship. Can he hold her with open arms?

Some say this is a love story with a mystery in the background. And it's a story of family and friendship as newlyweds Margaret and Max continue to be a meaningful part of Savannah's and Michael's world.

**Sleight of Paw (Book Three)**

In this story, Michael Ivey, the local veterinarian (Savannah's new husband) is attacked by an enraged client and then later accused of this man's murder. The evidence quickly stacks up against Michael, until Rags, Savannah's kleptomaniac cat, starts digging up clues implicating the unlikely suspect.

Coinciding with the details of this challenge is the discovery that the old house, which the couple purchased from Savannah's aunt, is cursed. Is this why the couple has not been blessed with a child?

Savannah's sister Brianna comes for a visit. She teams up with the Iveys' vet tech, Bud, to discover how to break the gypsy spell and they fall hard for each other. Will their courtship be strengthened or weakened by a frightening carjacking incident?

Detective Craig Sledge is prominent in this story as the lead investigator in the murder case. As usual, he engages in some creative tactics to get the information and the confessions he's after. He has also become embedded in Savannah's friend, Iris's family. He's dating Iris and helping with her son, Damon's rehabilitation in prison. If you read the 2nd in the series, you know that Rags (the cat) helped to put Damon in jail.


**Undercover Cat (Book Four)**

A popular local journalist goes missing just before she has the opportunity to turn in her story exposing unscrupulous cat hoarders. Not only is Colbi a friend of Savannah's and Michael's, Damon (now out of prison and employed by the local newspaper) has a strong personal interest in her. In fact, Damon breaks some rules and some trusts in his search for Colbi.

Is this a love connection? It's doubtful because Colbi is a strong advocate for the feral cat population and Damon hates cats—or so he believes.

Colbi's rescue is almost too late. She needs time to heal both physically and emotionally. So the Iveys invite her to recuperate in their home. Just when Colbi begins to feel safe, a body is discovered in the Iveys' orchard and Rags (their kleptomaniac cat) goes missing. Can someone in a nearby homeless camp shed some light on the evolving mystery?

**The Colony Cat Caper (Book Five)**
Savannah Ivey, a veterinarian out on maternity leave; her aunt Margaret, the founder of the Hammond Cat Alliance; and Colbi Stanton, a reporter for the local newspaper take on a cat colony at an old, abandoned building. Odd activity around the place makes them wonder if it actually is vacant; some believe it's occupied by something other-worldly.

When a stranger comes to town and suggests the Alliance open the old building to a fund-raiser, everyone gets involved, including Rags, Savannaha's kleptomaniac cat. He finds something that day that stirs a lot of people—both law-abiding and crooks—into action. Are the feral cats and their caretakers in serious danger? What (or who) lurks inside the old building? What secrets does It hide? And who has the key that unlocks the mystery?

**Celebrity Cat Caper (Book Six)**
Rags, the kleptomaniac cat, opens up a whole new bag of tricks, when he becomes a therapy cat in a children's reading program. A documentary film crew arrives to capture the cat

in action and they get more than they bargained for. Find out how Rags handles his sudden celebrity status.

In this story, Savannah and Michael Ivey invite strangers into their home during a torrential rainstorm and learn that one of them has a sinister past. Someone is murdered, Savannah is stalked, Michael's life is threatened, and Rags helps to uncover an old mystery that, until now, has everyone baffled.

The Iveys' baby Lily is three-and-a-half-months old and, along with nine-year-old Adam, provides some sweet and warm moments throughout this fast-moving story with many twists and turns.


**The Corral Cat Caper (Book Seven)**

Savannah Ivey's horse goes missing and Rags, the klepto cat, goes into mourning. Savannah and her friends spend days on horseback searching for Peaches over miles of dense wilderness. Along with a few dead-end clues, they stumble upon Elsie, a most unusual elderly woman living under dangerously primitive conditions. Elsie harbors secrets—some of which may lead to the recovery of Savannah's horse, but only after Rags puts his claws into the matter and Detective Craig Sledge gets involved.

*The Corral Cat Caper* features a lot of horse energy. It's rich in adventure of the feline as well as equine sort. In one scene, Rags attempt to save their sweet kitty, Buffy, from a catnapper and Savannah helplessly watches this drama unfold via a surveillance camera app on her phone.

This story is full of sweet and evil surprises, unexpected twists and turns, and plenty of action and adventure.

**Mansion of Meows (Book Nine)**

Rags's documentary is scheduled to debut. The showing will take place at the investor's San Francisco mansion, where the Ivey family and film crew will stay. Of course, the mansion holds secrets and Rags is instrumental in letting the cats out of the bag.

Savannah and Aunt Margaret share another daring adventure and, of course, find themselves in deeper than they expected.

This mystery may be the most eerie in the Klepto Cat Mystery series.

Made in the USA
Middletown, DE
11 August 2018